"An Earth-loving, spirit-touched book, warmly and lucidly accessible in its call to an ecological Christianity. It dreams of and defines a needed vision of our place and hope, our possibilities and accountabilities, among fellow earth creatures."

Catherine Keller
Drew University

"Hendrix College professor McDaniel, influenced by process theology and open to pluralism, critiques Christianity and then proposes an original application of ecological thought. While he savors some challenges to the roots of Christianity itself, he tends to be most at home with notions that are consistent with Christian ones, revised. The author's participation in ecumenical and interreligious activities informs this thoughtful book. Especially valuable is the annotated bibliography. We recommend this book for classroom and parish discussion groups, since McDaniel outlines and pursues his points clearly."

*The Christian Century*

"Jay B. McDaniel succeeds in synthesizing core insights of feminism, liberation theology, creation theology, and world religions and in focusing this varied knowledge 'round the central theme of an ecologically sound and nurturing faith.' The work is strengthened by provocative study questions, an insightful appendix on the role of silence in ecological spirituality, and a comprehensive, annotated bibliography."

*Doctrine & Life*

"Jay McDaniel 'attempts to articulate one version of an ecological Christianity that is open to all horizons of human life, other religions, and infused with a desire to affirm our inseparability from the natural world.' In it, various strands of contemporary theology—including process, feminist, liberation, and creation theology and world religions—are woven together in relation to the central theme of an ecologically sound and nurturing faith."

*One World*

"In the introduction, Professor McDaniel explains his ecological spirituality as one that assumes Christianity is, or can be, a way that excludes no ways, one that can be radically open to goodness wherever it is found. In new and unfamiliar ways I was encouraged to accept the universe, and more particularly, Earth as God's body; to see the beauty in the gods and goddesses of other religions, to affirm the cancer cell and the malaria-carrying mosquito as subjects of divine love and empathy; and to trust a God who can't prevent evil, but instead heals and resurrects. Though I find the book's message unconventional and disconcerting and related to New Age thinking, there were some ideas worth pondering."

*The Living Church*

"Capitalizing on widespread concern for ecology, Jay B. McDaniel argues persuasively that Christianity frees us to say yes to life in its fullness. In his foreword, Rev. Thomas Berry, 'the most visionary ecological theologian' or geologian of today, insists that our human well-being is inseparable from that of Earth's.

"McDaniel speaks of God as a lure, a beckoning presence, leading us to the fullest expression of our lives as persons respectful of ourselves, of others, and of our environment. As part of a single web of existence, he believes we must be committed 'to a world that is more socially just, more ecologically sustainable, and more spiritually satisfying for all.'"

*Prairie Messenger*

Foreword by THOMAS BERRY

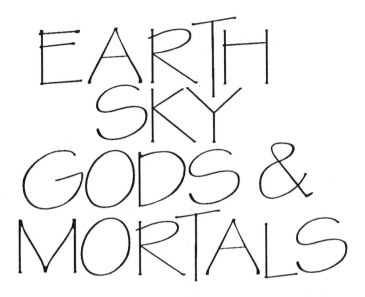

# EARTH SKY GODS & MORTALS

## A Theology of Ecology for the 21st Century

## JAY B. McDANIEL

TWENTY-THIRD PUBLICATIONS
Mystic, Connecticut 06355

**Third printing 1994**

Twenty-Third Publications
P.O. Box 180
185 Willow Street
Mystic, CT 06355
(203) 536-2611
(800) 321-0411

ISBN 0-89622-412-0
Library of Congress Catalog Card No. 89-51581
Printed in the U.S.A.

# Foreword

The theological agenda, in this late twentieth century, is shifting to ecological issues. Jay McDaniel's *Earth, Sky, Gods, and Mortals: A Theology of Ecology for the 21st Century* is welcomed evidence of this.

This shift toward ecological issues can be observed in all phases of the human endeavor. In economics the most significant question of the future is not the national debt of some four trillion dollars, or the annual budgetary deficit of over one hundred billion dollars, or the trade deficit of another hundred billion dollars; it is rather the ecological deficit, the decline in the gross Earth product.

So too in medicine. The basic issue is the ecological issue, the health of the planet as the condition for any integral development of human health. It is beginning to dawn on the medical profession that we cannot have well people on a sick planet. To continue countering biological deterioration with manipulative technologies will never work.

So too in the other professions. In law our greatest need presently is new legal structures dealing with the relations between humans and Earth, interspecies law, not simply interhuman law. As regards national security, the basic issue is no longer military security but ecological security. Political refugees are now giving way to ecological refugees, peoples whose land has become desert or otherwise too depleted in its fertility to continue supporting its human population.

The next generation needs to be educated for life within the community of life systems, not simply for life within the human community. Youth needs to become literate in the Great Book of Nature as well as in books written by humans. Indeed, all the great books composed by humans were themselves evoked by experiences of the natural world about us.

If these observations have at least some validity, we can immediately perceive how important is our religious interaction with the natural world. If the waters of the world become polluted they can neither be drunk for physical refreshment nor can they be used for baptism since they have become symbols of death rather than of life. So too with the air; if the air becomes toxic it no longer can bear the symbolism of the Holy Spirit. Nor can the mountains or rivers or the seas speak to us of the ultimate grandeur of existence. We lose a profound spiritual experience if we can no longer observe the butterfly as it moves from its larval stage to its cocoon to emerge in the magnificence of its colorful flight.

Already our spiritual experience is severely attenuated because of our insensitivity to the diminishment of the natural world that is taking place in our industrial civilization. Our children will live in a world less resplendent than the world we have lived in. Development of their inner psychic life will be correspondingly difficult. Even now we are losing fifty acres of rainforest  every minute of every day, rainforests that are perhaps the most magnificent expression of life in the universe.

The tragedy is that our religious and spiritual traditions have been so insensitive to these happenings. The pathos of the human has taken our attention in recent decades. Now, however, it is clear that the destiny of humans cannot be separated from the destiny of Earth. If we continue to lose, in the United States, some four to six billion tons of topsoil annually, the time will come when we will be unable to feed more than a portion of the people dependent on the food grown there.

However the situation has been in the past, the situation now is clear. We must move beyond a spirituality focused simply on the divine and the human to a spirituality concerned with survival of the natural world in its full splendor, its fertility, and its integral well-being as the larger spiritual community to which we belong. The Earth community is the larger dimension of our own being; for we have not only our individual self, but also our family self, our community self, our human self, our Earth self, and eventually our universe self. Our integral self has all these aspects.

Each of these has its sacred dimension. Indeed, nothing is itself in any adequate manner without everything else. Humans are an abstraction if we think of ourselves separate from the air and the water and sunshine and the soil under our feet. If we exploit and diminish Earth, we exploit and diminish our own being. We lose the deepest psychic and spiritual modalities of our existence.

That we should not have developed a more effective religious interpretation of the emergent universe reveals the impoverishment of our traditions. At the same time, our present experience should be awakening us to a new sense of the role we are being called to in guiding the course of the future. A vast amount of social disruption must take place as we move away from our present industrial economy. We need the entrancing vision of a more integral life situation if we are to undertake the transformation needed.

New religious sensitivities need to emerge, not from any traditional verbal revelation or traditional text, but from our present experience of a developmental universe known by empirical observation as both a psychic-spiritual as well as a physical-material reality from its beginning. This experience itself can be considered as revelatory, although it is of a different order and does not replace the earlier revelations that have guided religious life in the past.

If for some time science abandoned the spiritual dimension of the universe to penetrate as deeply as possible into the material structure of the world, this effort has ended in a realization that there is no such thing as crass matter. There is no objective world such as this has been conceived in the past; there is only the world of spirit-matter. There is a consciousness dimension, a subjectivity, a self at every level of existence, a sacred aspect.

All this is now beginning to be understood as the new religious agenda begins to find expression. So here in this study, *Earth, Sky, Gods, and Mortals* by Jay McDaniel, we find a new context for an ecological theology and spirituality. In a remarkable way he has brought together the traditional modes of religious thought with the modern scientific insights and the philosophy of organism proposed by Alfred North Whitehead, all as aspects of an integral approach to our ecological concerns. I am myself especially impressed with his discussion of Whitehead, whose thought is so basic in bringing about a creative response to our present situation.

As a final comment I would observe that in recent years a vast change of consciousness seems to be sweeping over the entire human community, a change in all our professions and institutions, a change away from our plundering industrial order to a functional ecological order. We begin to realize that we are members not simply of a human community but of a larger community, the multi-species community, that encompasses the entire world of the living and indeed the entire complex of all those beings that constitute our homeland planet, Earth.

Thomas Berry

# Acknowledgments

This book attempts to articulate one version of an ecological Christianity that is open to all horizons of human life, open to other religions, and infused with a desire to affirm our inseparability from the natural world. This is no small order. Even if articulated by one person, it must be a synthesis of many voices and many ideas. Theology, too, is an act of affirming connections with others, of learning from their criticisms, and of synthesizing ideas they have offered.

My own theology in this book is no exception. It will quickly become clear that my version of an ecological Christianity is deeply indebted to several thinkers in a contemporary theological movement called "process theology." This school of thought, whose history began at the University of Chicago in the 1930s, provides the general framework for the synthesis I undertake. Still, the book is truly the result of many voices, including many who are not influenced at all by process theology. Sometimes the voices have been critical, sometimes constructive; always they have been helpful. Besides the more academic influences, I would like to mention a few of the more personal voices that indirectly speak in this book.

They include many of my students past and present, not least of whom are Len and Beka Miles-Deloney, who met each other in a class I taught on process theology, and who showed me that a process theology divorced from liberation concerns is radically insufficient for our times. These voices also include the helpful ideas and criticisms of many colleagues at Hendrix College, particularly Francis Christie, John Churchill, Bland Crowder, Bill

Eakin, Peg Falls-Corbitt, John Farthing, Cathy Goodwin, Jon Guthrie, Lawrence Schmidt, Gary Valen, and Cullen Weeden. I am especially indebted to Cathy Goodwin and Cullen Weeden, not only for insights that feed into the content, but for help in preparing the manuscript amid its countless revisions.

Influential voices in this book also include friends at the Meadowcreed Project, an environmental education organization in Fox, Arkansas, on whose Board of Directors I sit. In this regard special thanks go to the project's founders: David Orr, who showed me how important "openness to the earth" must be for a viable Christianity, and who introduced me to the thought of Thomas Berry, Wendell Berry, Wes Jackson, Amory Lovins, and to his own thought. Thanks go also to Wilson Orr, whose appreciation of the importance of rural community has shown me that an "openness to the earth" must include openness to those in rural settings whose lives are so closely bound to the earth.

Voices present in this work also include friends and colleagues from outside my immediate environs, such as Kevin Clark, Rita Brock, Michael Cartwright, Paula Cooey, Sheila Davaney, Catherine Keller, Nancy Howell, Les Muray, Charles Pinches, David Pipes, and Norbert Schedler, whose points of view have shaped my own perspective in many important ways. I would like to offer a special word of thanks to Kevin and Les, who are my regular roommates and theological soul-mates at the annual meeting of the American Academy of Religion, and who have so often expressed more confidence in me than I deserve. Voices in this book also include my teacher and friend John B. Cobb, Jr., whose example and intellectual guidance have shown me that Christianity can be a way of openness and adventure, and whose encouragement has given me the motivation to write this book. And they include Charles Birch, whose book, *The Liberation of Life*, co-authored with John Cobb, has played a central role in my own way of thinking, and whose friendship I have enjoyed through our mutual work with the World Council of Churches.

Another influential voice in this book is Roshi Keido

Another influential voice in this book is Roshi Keido Fukushima, Zen Master at Tofukuji Monastery in Kyoto, Japan, whose free mind has both shown me the truth of Buddhist non-attachment and the truth of Buddhist compassion. In helping me to understand Buddhism, Dr. Margaret Dornish of Pomona College in Claremont, California, has also been an indispensable inspiration.

Many of the voices in this book are relatives. They include my cousin John McDaniel Wheeler, with whom I have had numerous immensely rewarding discussions at an isolated, corrugated-metal cabin in a pine forest near Chidester, Arkansas, and whose stories, love of nature, love of family, and concern for the forgotten are a veritable model of an integrative spirituality. They include my father- and mother-in-law, Art and Martha Johnson, who have shown me how spiritually enriching a scientifically-informed appreciation of nature can be. Thanks to them, I have come to see ornithology as a spiritual discipline in its own right. They include my sister and brother-in-law, Linda and Ian Schulze, whose continued support of me and my family and whose love for their own children show me just how important Christian family life can be to the ecological path. Thanks to them—and to their daughters Suzanne, Beth, and Cynda—I have come to see that there can be much spirituality in mutually encouraging family relationships. They include my son Jason, whose laughter, tears, and openness to fresh possibilities remind me how beautifully two-year-olds can bear witness to God's presence. And they include my wife Kathy, whose sensitivity to all things living, whose strength of character, whose kindness and sense of humor, to me are continual inspirations.

I dedicate this book to two additional relatives who speak through these pages. One is my father, John B. McDaniel, Jr., whose times spent with me on the banks and in the water of the Guadalupe River near Hunt, Texas, gave me my earliest and most imporant spiritual experiences with nature; whose business skills and fatherly care made it possible for me to go to school, and hence develop the skills to theologize about those experiences; and whose vision led to the construction of that isolated cabin in Chidester, Arkansas, mentioned above, where I still gain so much spiritual nourishment. The other is my mother, Virginia C. McDaniel, whose continual encouragement gave me confidence to write what follows; whose listening ear showed me what openness to other people can really mean; whose comments, advice, and perspectives shaped many of my ideas; and whose compassion and open-minded spirit, like that of my father, show me that Christianity can be, after all, a Way that excludes no ways.

# CONTENTS

# Introduction

Some students of mine, many mathematics and physics majors, read large amounts of science fiction in their spare time. They enjoy exploring worlds that exist in a realm of pure possibility, worlds that might exist and perhaps even ought to exist, but that are different from the world we know. With their vivid imaginations and heightened propensities for enjoying sheer possibilities, these students exemplify what in this work I call a "spirituality of the sky." Other students, many of them biology majors, are more down-to-earth. In their spare time they would rather roam in the woods looking for insects under dead logs, or stare at the intricate beauty of a dragonfly wing, than scan the horizons of pure possibility. They exemplify what I call a "spirituality of the earth" combined with an openness to plants and animals, which is one feature of what I call a "spirituality of mortals."

Still other students, many of them majoring in one of the social sciences or the humanities, are more people-centered. In their spare time they would rather sit over coffee in the student union talking with friends about current affairs, or in a dorm at two in the morning sharing their respective hopes and dreams for the future, than walk in the woods looking at insects. They, too, exemplify a "spirituality of mortals," but in this instance the mortals are other humans.

Finally, there are still others, oftentimes psychology or literature majors, who are more introspective in disposition. In their spare time they would prefer to write poetry that expresses the feelings and moods of their inner lives, or survey the world's mythologies for parallels to their own dreams, than socialize with people about public affairs. They find their meaning in the realm of internal images and archetypes, and in so doing exemplify what I call a "spirituality of the gods."

Most people, my students and I included, find meaning in one or several of these spiritualities. We may be people-centered with a penchant for the sky, or earth-centered with a penchant for the gods, or we may even exemplify a healthy balance of openness to the earth, sky, gods, and mortals. Unfortunately, most us have not been taught by our churches to think of our sources of daily nourishment as particularly "religious""or "spiritual." At least this is the case with most of my students. For them, the religion they know best is Protestant Christianity of a Bible-belt variety. "Religion" is primarily about going to church, believing in God, and living a good life, and "spirituality" is primarily about praying before meals and after temptation. Christianity has nothing to do with science fiction, dragonfly wings, bull sessions at two in the morning, or the writing of poetry.

I am not comfortable with this compartmentalization of Christianity to a private sphere of personal belief and church worship. Neither are most of my students who profess Christianity. Though we have not been taught in church to think of our most cherished, daily activities as "spiritualities," we would like to think of them this way. We would like to think that the writing of poetry, even bad poetry, involves the lure of God; that the enjoyment of science fiction is one way of discovering the divine Intelligence; that listening to another person share her or his dreams is one way of communing with the divine Dreamer; and that delight in the intricacy of a dragonfly wing is one way of sharing divine Delight. We would like to think that Christianity frees us to say "yes" to life in its fullness.

But even this is not enough. As we learn about other religions, doing our best to place ourselves empathetically inside Buddhist, Hindu, Jewish, Muslim and other religious perspectives, we become increasingly dissatisfied with the exclusivism that has been part of the Christian heritage. The Christianity we seek must not be a belief system that closes us off from other religions, but rather a way of life, a way that excludes no ways, at least those that can enrich our own capacities for love and compassion. Our Christianity must not only encourage an openness to the earth, sky, gods, and mortals; it must also encourage an openness to other paths.

And even this is not enough. As we study Third World liberation theologies, or feminist and black theologies in North America, we realize that our Christianity must be challenging. Even as it opens us to the insights of other religious paths, it must also challenge us to hear deeply the voices of the poor, the marginalized, the outcast, and the victimized, and to let their desires for wholeness become our own. It must force us to recognize our own complicity in unjust social orders, and to repent of our own absorption in the greed and self-indulgence of a consumer society. It must help us to combine a "yes" to the earth, sky, gods, and mortals, and a "yes" to other religions, with a "no" to the tragic injustices of our times, so many of which are the product of our own hands.

Moreover, Christianity must help us say "no" to the widespread destruction of the natural world of which we are a part, and to the widespread abuse of individual animals in factory farms, scientific laboratories, and other areas of animal subjugation. The Christianity we seek must extend the concept of liberation to include the earth itself and other animals. The Way that excludes no ways must not focus on justice for humans alone, but rather on justice for all living beings too. It must enable us to say "yes" to the healing powers of nature itself, and thereby to live lives of deep-seated respect for life and environment.

Why do many of us experience this need? I suggest that it is because, today, many of us find ourselves in the "third phase" of a Christian religious journey.

## The Third-Phase Christian

As Dorothee Soelle and Shirley Cloyes explain, the first phase occurred during childhood when we, as Christians, were "socialized to the religious norms, beliefs, and practices of our ancestors."[1] This was the religion of our upbringing, our home town, of what Soelle calls our "isolated childhood village." For many of us this religious way was rich and meaningful. It consisted of deeply held beliefs combined with prayer and, for some, regular church attendance. It offered security amid uncertainty, hope amid despair, trust amid doubt.

Yet the first phase was also naive. We had not yet discovered that many of our inherited beliefs could not stand the tests of reason and experience. We had not seen, for example, that our convictions concerning an all-loving and all-powerful God could not easily be reconciled, or perhaps reconciled at all, with the immensity of worldly suffering. Nor had we encountered the reality of religious pluralism, and seen that a traditional theology of exclusivism, in which Christ is proclaimed as the only way, is arrogant and uncompassionate in a world of pluralism, a world in which there are many worthwhile religious ways. Nor had we internalized global consciousness, and recognized that many of the urgent social problems we face today—problems of war and the threat of nuclear holocaust, of social injustice, and of ecological unsustainability—are partly caused by Christianity itself.

The second phase occurred as a result of the above-mentioned realizations, or at least of realizations like them. With the gradual discovery and partial mastery of that "critical reason" so celebrated in Western education, we saw the faults and problems of our "village" religion. As Soelle and Cloyes put it, we moved to the city, "if not in actuality, then in our imaginations." Some of us abandoned prayer and attending church. Religion, with Christianity as its model, either drifted into the background of our lives as a forgotten frame of reference, or it was painfully recalled as a burden wrongly imposed in childhood to be persistently exorcised. We lived as post-Christian inhabitants of the secular city. Critical reason became the object of our faith; secular humanism, in which reference to God or the Holy is deemed irrelevant, became our creed.

Just as some people have stayed in the first phase all their lives, so some have remained in the second phase. Indeed, many in the twentieth- century West have been reared in a second-phase way of thinking, avoiding the first phase altogether. They have been brought up as modern heirs of the seventeenth- and eighteenth-century Western Enlightenment. The truths of science, not those of religion, are their guide. For them, the second phase is not a transition to something further, it is the very norm for an authentic life.

Nonetheless, some have moved on to a third phase. We have done so for different reasons, but almost always as a result of our feeling that the second phase, with its stress on critical reason and secular humanism, lacked a depth dimension, a sense of mystery, an awareness of the Holy, and a sense of connectedness with all that is. From a third-phase perspective, the second phase failed to recognize that, after all, humans are part of a larger cosmic, and even divine, story. Without a feeling for this larger story, humanism itself becomes arrogant, wrongly proffering a philosophy that humans are the measure of all things. Those of us who entered the third phase have retained our appreciation of critical reason, but we have moved beyond secular humanism "in search of sacred ground." In this context many of us reconsidered and in time reappropriated Christianity. We became third-phase Christians.[2]

Some of us in the third phase do in fact attend church and even pray again. We recognize that we cannot be Christians without the help of others who are similarly committed, and that the Christian life is best nourished by fellowship and community. But, in the words of Soelle and Cloyes, we "will not allow religious authoritarianism to hamstring our lives." As third-phase Christians we understand our lives as open-ended journeys in which we seek, not certainty or an end to ambiguity, but rather depth, breadth, and meaning. We realize that the pilgrimage is ongoing, that in matters of ultimate importance absolute certainty is unattainable and perhaps undesirable, and that change is to be expected. It is *amid* this process of change, not apart from it, that we seek that sacred ground by which life is enriched and existence sustained. In traditional Christian language, we seek the living God.

What is it like to find God? Certainly it is not to possess God as an object of knowledge, a reified set of doctrinal propositions. Nor is it to enter into a state of self-assured certainty concerning the finality of one's beliefs. Rather it is to find God in many ways that elude rigid compartmentalization in doctrine. It is to find God, vaguely and tentatively, in prayer and meditation, in other people and in fellow creatures, in the earth and in the sky, in solitude and in communion. When third-phase Christians find God in these ways and places, we live what can be called a *t*hird-phase, ecological Christianity.

The type of Christianity we seek is "ecological" in two senses. First, even as it is tenaciously committed to peace and justice among humans, it presupposes and affirms the continuity of human with nonhuman life, refusing to separate the religious life from a commitment to the flourishing of life, nonhuman as well as human. Second, just as ecological studies in biology emphasize the interconnectedness of organisms with their environments, so the third-phase spirituality we seek takes the fact of our connectedness with the entire range of existence, and with God, as the heart of Christian spirituality. It is a worldly spirituality, one that finds God in the enjoyment of rich relations to the entire range of existence.

## The Entire Range of Existence

Borrowing from the philosopher Martin Heidegger and adapting his idea to different purposes, I suggest that the "entire range of existence" includes the earth, the sky, the gods, and other mortals.[3] By "earth" I mean our terrestrial home, including its material formations, the most immediate of which are our own bodies. When we are attuned to the earth, we appreciate the beauty, strength, and fragility of the finite, using earthly materials in a kindly way and appreciating them in their own intrinsic value. By "sky" I mean the earth's home, the heavens beneath which we stand. Attuned to the sky, we sense the presence of the unbounded and unlimited, recognizing our own finitude and also encountering a realm of pure possibility by which our imaginations can be inspired and our hopes stimulated. By "gods" I mean those internal apparitions—be they gods, goddesses, or other kinds of spirits—that we discover, among other places, within our own psyches in dreams and fantasies. In touch with them, we recognize that there are dimensions other than that of external sense perception with which we are deeply connected, and that in these domains we may well discover aspects of ourselves and of God otherwise neglected. Lastly, by "mortals" I mean those creatures with whom we share the reality of biological life: other humans, other animals, and plants. Realizing our connectedness with mortals, we discover possibilities for care, justice, intimacy, trust, and communion which are not possible in any of the other spheres.

With its emphasis on relatedness to the earth, sky, gods, and mortals, my hope is that this book provides an alternative to that retreat from openness which characterizes much Christian thinking in our time. Amid its openness, however, this spirituality must involve a spirit of self-criticism and tentativeness. If we follow this way, we ought not absolutize our own theology or our own spirituality as if it were the only genuine path to follow. After all, the living God cannot be exhausted in particular theologies or a particular spirituality. This means that not all ecological "third-phase" Christians ought necessarily adopt my description of an ecological spirituality. I am describing *one version* of such a spirituality; there can and should be many versions. It means, in addition, that not all Christians need such a spirituality at all. Some people may indeed be called by God toward more conservative forms of thinking: that is, toward forms of thinking that are more richly tied to past forms of Christian thought than is the one to be adumbrated. Finally, it means that an ecological spirituality such as I describe may itself be limited to a Western cultural pattern. When we recall that today more than fifty percent of the Christians in the world live in Asia, Africa, Latin America, and Oceania, we realize that non-Western Christians may undergo quite different, and equally legitimate, stages of faith.

## A Pluralistic Age

As the comments above suggest, we live not only in an "ecological nuclear age," as Sallie McFague phrases it, but also in a pluralistic age. While my version of an ecological spirituality is *explicitly* Christian, it is not *exclusively* Christian. The reason for this is twofold. First, the spiritual sensitivities to be described can well be embodied by people who are not Christian. Be they practitioners of primal traditions, healthy agnostics, radical feminists, Hindus, Buddhists, Jews, or Muslims, their embodiment of the traits to be described can be celebrated rather than bemoaned. From the Christian perspective I attempt to express, authentic spirituality is not the exclusive domain of Christians. Those of us in the Christian community can fittingly celebrate plurality and differences among persons, but we can also rightly celebrate commonalities with those who travel different paths when such commonalities are apparent.

Second, the ecological spirituality to be described is not exclusively Christian because the sensitivities that inform it can be cultivated, by Christians themselves, through an internalization of insights from non-Christian sources. Indeed, I draw heavily from Buddhism to articulate a "faith without absolutes" in Chapter Two, and then from Hinduism to discuss openness to the gods and goddesses in Chapter Six. The Christians to whom this work speaks are not content to rely solely on the Christian past as a resource for understanding what it means to be a Christian in the present and near future. We realize that we exist in an emerging global culture, and that there are manifold resources outside the Christian heritage that are relevant to a Christian understanding of both God and the world. For us, to be fully Christian is not to be closed to the world. Rather it is to be fully open to the world, learning from others and trusting that, wherever there is truth, there is the very God in whom we believe as Christians. This spirituality is one that assumes Christianity is, or can be, a Way that excludes no ways.

By "a Way that excludes no ways" I do not mean a Way that is tolerant of *everything*. We must resist many evils in our world. We ought not be tolerant of our destruction of the earth, of our oppression of the poor, of our abuse of animals, of our violence, of our impatience with those we love, or of our incessant cravings for instant gratification. Nor ought we be tolerant of our own bigoted intolerance. Still, there is much in the world that, even when riddled with ambiguity, is worthy of tolerance and appreciation: the goodness we find in other religions, in animals, in the earth itself. To say that Christianity is, or can be, a Way that excludes no ways is to say that it can be radically open to goodness wherever it is found, even if found in new and unfamiliar places.

The idea that the Christian life is, or can be, a way of openness to the new and unfamiliar is at the heart of this work. Yet it is *not* an idea that I attempt to defend on systematic grounds. Rather, it is an assumption with which I begin. The assumption has already been defended and amplified, to my mind successfully, by John B. Cobb, Jr. in his *Christ in a Pluralistic Age*. Indeed, the phrase "a Way that excludes no ways" comes from Cobb's introduction to that work, where he writes:

Today...we find ourselves together on a limited and endangered planet we have learned to think of as Spaceship Earth. At the moment of our recognition of how great the threat of our own actions pose to that spaceship, we also see more clearly than ever before how deep are the divisions that separate our communities from one another, how confused and confusing are the voices that would direct our management of the spaceship, how widespread is our sense of impotence and futility, and how lacking we are collectively in relevant, creative vision. The question the Christian hears in this situation is whether there is a way through the chaos of our time so that we can be brought together with others rather than try to run rough-shod over them. *This book proposes that for us Christ is the Way that excludes no ways.*[4]

The Christian perspective that I develop here takes as its point of departure Cobb's understanding of Christ.

Cobb is a process theologian influenced both by biblical points of view and by the philosophical perspectives of Alfred North Whitehead and Charles Hartshorne. Cobb's is a *process* understanding of Christ, which is to say that he understands Christ as that living Spirit—that divine Logos—by whom con-temporary Christians and others are beckoned, not toward a changeless mode of existence, but rather toward a life that is characterized by ongoing openness to new possibilities derived from God. For him we experience Christ as a divine beckoning toward creative transformation relative to the circumstances at hand. Such transformation can rightly occur through openness to people of other faiths, as well as to nonhuman animals and the earth.

With its emphasis on openness to the new and unfamiliar, the process-oriented, ecological Christian perspective of this work partly mirrors and partly diverges from the Christian past. Throughout its history Christianity has absorbed and been transformed by alien ideas and insights. Biblical traditions were influenced by Mesopotamian, Persian, Egyptian, Greek, and Ro-man perspectives; apostolic and medieval Christians by Greek perspectives; modern Christians by indigenous traditions from Asia, Africa, and Latin America. It is one thing to be influenced by alien ideas, however, and another to acknowledge that influ-ence once it has occurred, and to seek out further examples of it. Such acknowledgment and openness have indeed been seen in some but not all periods of the Christian past. Clement of Alexandria welcomed Greek influence; Tertullian disdained it. Aquinas also welcomed it; but Luther loathed it. My concern that Christians be transformed by insights from Buddhism, Hinduism, and other sources falls in the tradition of Clement and Aquinas.

But in this work I do not consciously seek to be traditional. I do not begin with the assumption that authentic Christian thinking is necessarily repetitious of, or revisionary of, traditional Christian views, biblical or post-biblical. Rather, I assume that authentic Christian thinking is responsive to an inwardly felt and divinely derived call to recognize truth, goodness, and beauty wherever they are found. Christians are those who believe that this call was embodied decisively, though not exclusively, in Jesus Christ, and thus that Jesus serves as a key to understanding the call. We believe that the call was a word which became flesh in a young Jew from Nazareth. Yet we recognize that Jesus himself did not exhaust the word. The word continues as a voice—a lure—to which all of us can respond. With Cobb, I call this lure the living Christ. It is my hope that this work, traditional or not, is responsive to the word become flesh.

## CHAPTER ONE

# Ecological Thinking
# and the Future

"World War III has begun! Beware of victory!" So read the placard held by an elderly Native American man dressed in traditional attire, who was standing outside the gates of the White House one spring several years ago. He was one among several protesters in front of the White House that day, each advocating a cause. A group of tourists on its way to the National Gallery of Art walked up to him, and I was among them. We asked him who was fighting World War III.

"The war is against the earth," he said, "and we are fighting it. You and I and everybody. Almost everything we do is part of the war. We're winning it in the Third World. We're destroying the rainforests and washing away the soils. We're winning it in the First and Second Worlds, too, by poisoning our rivers and atmospheres. The earth is strong, but we'll proceed with the war anyway. Even if it takes nuclear war. This is why I'm holding this sign. I'm protesting the war."

As we walked on, we knew that the man was right. We felt that we should have been standing alongside him. For we humans *are* engaged in a sustained, ongoing war against the earth. The privileged and powerful among us fight the war out of choice; the poor and powerless out of necessity. The victims of the war include other species, whose rates of extinction are unparalleled in the earth's history: one a day at present, and perhaps 130 a day by the turn of the century. They include individual animals subjected to cruel treatment in factory farming, scientific experimentation, and the testing of consumer goods and cosmetics. And, not least, they include countless of our own sisters and brothers, countless people. For the practices which support a war against the earth also support a war against the poor. When hundreds of thousands of people are dying from too little to eat, such that they have to cut down precious forests just to survive, and others are dying from too much to eat, there is something wrong with our whole way of thinking and acting. Somehow we must learn to walk more lightly on the earth, and more justly with one another, both for the earth's sake and for our own.

An ecological spirituality must therefore begin where this protestor began, and where many native Americans and others of primal traditions begin. It must begin with a protest against the current battle of humans against one another and the earth, and with a hope for a lasting peace on earth, a peace among humans and between humans and the earth. The emergence of this peace will have to involve a new way of thinking and feeling among religious peoples. We can best get at this new way of thinking by assessing various possibilities for the human future.

## Images of the Future

As a single human family inhabiting a small and fragile planet in a backwater galaxy, what *is* our future? One to two hundred years from now, in what kind of world will people find themselves? Gary Coates, architect and pioneer in the environmental movement, suggests four images, some hopeful and some not.[1]

First, there is the image of *a superindustrial future* offered by technological optimists. Here we have a world heavily influenced by the blessings, though not the liabilities, of advanced science. Poverty and disease have been eliminated, urban affluence abounds, and outer space is being explored as the final and perhaps the most exciting of human frontiers. An infinite supply of energy has been made available through nuclear power, and ten to fifteen billion people earn the equivalent of $40,000 a year enjoying a "technotopia" of manufactured fun and adventure.

Second, and again on the optimistic side from the point of view of its advocates, is the possibility of *an environmentally attuned future* proposed by feminist thinkers and by some environmentalists. In this scenario, environmental activists have won the battle against nuclear power; ecologically-conscious economists have shown us how to transcend earlier commitments to unlimited economic growth; politicians have helped us to distribute our scarce resources equitably; small-scale communities have recovered the lost arts of local self-reliance; and, particularly emphasized by feminists, patriarchal modes of governance and thought have been replaced by partnership and holistic thinking. Emphasis has been placed on spiritual growth rather than physical growth, on quality rather than quantity, on life rather than things. Rather than a technotopia of fun and adventure, we have an "ecotopia" of symbiotic relationships between self, nature, and society.

Third, and markedly more pessimistic than the first two, is the possibility of *a totalitarian future*. Here we have a world dominated by a single world government or by a consortium of iron governments, each attempting to maintain social order in the face of diminishing supplies of natural resources. The world is ruled by managerial, technological, and military elites who severely minimize the liberty of their subjects in order to maximize possibilities for general survival. Democracy is remembered as a failed experiment, or totalitarianism is itself called democracy. Neither a technotopia of abundance nor an ecotopia of communion with nature, the totalitarian future is a "totalitopia": a repressive "place" in which Orwell's *Nineteen Eighty-Four* has been belatedly actualized.

Fourth, and even more pessimistic, is the possibility of a *future marked by limited nuclear war*. In this scenario, close to half the nuclear weapons of the superpowers have been fired for one reason or another. Hundreds of millions of immediate deaths have been caused by explosions, and a large but unknown number of subsequent deaths have been effected by fire and heat. Additional hundreds of millions of seriously injured survivors have died soon after the explosions. Many of the survivors are so incapacitated psychologically that they are unable to care for themselves. Water supplies have been poisoned, the soil is contaminated, disease and famine run rampant, and we find ourselves in a state of sheer chaos, a new and unprecedented Dark Age. A future of this sort is not a technotopia, an ecotopia, or a totalitopia. Perhaps it is best called a "dystopia": that socially dysfunctional and biologically dysgenic "place" that would follow a limited nuclear war.

The very existence of these four images shows us how uncertain we are. The future remains a mystery, unknown and unknowable, and the disparity of available images shows us how manifold are our possibilities. Moreover, the last two images—totalitopia and dystopia—remind us of the dangers we face. If, as the twentieth-century philosopher Alfred North Whitehead says, it is the business of the future to be dangerous, the future is indeed doing its business.

At this stage in history, however, such images can only be formed against the backdrop of a fifth possibility, the probability of which, like that of the other four, is difficult to assess. It is possible, for reasons that may or may not be beyond our ken, that nuclear arms may proliferate even beyond their present destructive power, and that the future would entail an all-out nuclear holocaust, in which the whole of humankind, perhaps even the whole of life, is destroyed. Along with the images of technotopia, ecotopia, totalitopia, and dystopia, then, we must add a final image to our imaginative reservoir: an "antitopia," a "placeless place" in which life itself, or at least human life, has been extinguished.

If we are to avoid some of the more negative scenarios just

identified, we need more than new forms of social organization and behavior, important as these are. We need, in addition, new, more "ecological" forms of thinking and new, more "ecological" forms of spirituality. These new forms can help us avoid the disasters of nuclear war, ecological collapse, and totalitarianism, and they can help us find our way toward what I will call "our best hope." In the remainder of this chapter I begin the task of describing such a spirituality by identifying and describing our best hope for the future, given that concern for the fullness of life which is central to a third-phase Christian faith described in the Introduction. After identifying this hope, I explain an "ecological" way of thinking which we might ourselves embody, if we, as travelers in the third phase, are to help make that hoped-for historical future a reality. Then I explain the role that our own spirituality, as lived in the present, might play in embodying that hoped-for future. The chapter is divided into three sections corresponding to these aims.

## The Best Hope

What if we fail to avoid the ultimate holocaust? Of course, we would not be the first in the history of our planet to perish. The fossil record shows that there have been many periods in which mass extinctions of large animal groups have occurred. Almost two-thirds of the small, crustacean-like trilobites disappeared at the end of the Cambrian Period 500 million years ago. At the close of the Permian Period 250 million years later, nearly half of the existing animal species became extinct. Some 65 million years ago the dinosaurs disappeared. Nuclear annihilation would be our occasion for joining the ranks of these exanimated groups, our own evolutionary ancestors.

Nevertheless, we would be the first among our fellow creatures to perish in such a violent and self-willed fashion, and to take so many along with us. Our own history would be over, and there would be none among us to tell the tale of our rise and fall. Just as the story of the dinosaurs, who dominated the earth for a 150 million years, can only be told by us, their nondinosauric successors, so our story, a much briefer one by reptilian standards, could only be told, if at all, by non-human successors.

## Shalom

What is our best hope? Biblical traditions sometimes call it "shalom." This Hebrew word, often translated "peace," means not simply the absence of violence, but rather the fullness of life. This fullness is not only for human beings, it is for all creatures in relation to one another. As Walter Brueggemann explains, "The central vision of world history in the Bible is that all of creation is one, every creature in community with every other, living in harmony and security toward the joy and well-being of every other creature."[2] Shalom is that harmony which would inform a community that has realized this vision. This harmony would be a feature of the communal order itself, and of the subjective lives of the individuals constituting that order. Shalom is harmony externally observed and internally felt.

In order to avoid unrealistic romanticism, it is important to draw a distinction between shalom as an ideal fully realized and shalom as an ideal to be ambiguously and tentatively approximated. As an ideal *fully* realized, shalom could be achieved, if at all, only in a plane of existence radically different from what we know as earthly, historical existence. Given predator-prey relations, for example, it is very difficult to image a state of affairs in which, as Brueggemann puts it, "every creature" lives "in harmony and security toward the joy and well-being of every other creature." There may be a kind of external "harmony" in the overall ecological system in which the wolf eats the rabbit, but it is doubtful that the rabbit feels this harmony from an internal perspective as she is being eaten. As long as even one rabbit experiences disharmony, the *fullness* of shalom has not been realized. In life as we know it, the fullness of shalom is an impossible ideal.

Realistically, then, our best hope is for approximations of shalom. In terms of the images noted in the previous section, it is for an approximation of ecotopia, combined with what is best, not worst, in the technotopian scenario. In this scenario we would have learned to use, responsibly, certain forms of advanced technology, and we would have learned to dwell sanely and humanely in relation to ourselves, our fellow humans, other animals, and nature. Our approximation would not be a state of blissful perfection. It would not be devoid of natural or moral evil. There would still be predator-prey relations, and for us there would still be unwanted suffering and untimely deaths. Our best hope is that there might be a minimization of those forms of evil and destruction for which we are ourselves responsible, and that amid this minimization there might also be, in degrees heretofore unrealized, ecstasy and trust, wholeness and solidarity.

## Global Village

The phrase "global village" can help us to elaborate further this hope. By global village I mean a worldwide community of communities, linked in many ways by advanced communication systems, in which various members enjoy certain forms of local autonomy even as they enjoy other forms of cooperative interdependence. Some of these communities may be nation- states; others may be bioregions; still others may be rural communities or cities. In identifying those communities which together constitute a global village, it is best to begin by looking to places where people already exist in some degree of solidarity with one another and with nature, even if those communities are nation-states. What is important, however, is always to keep in mind that the "communities" constituting a global village are themselves formed by the earth, plants, and nonhuman animals, as well as by people. Communities are both human and ecological. They are homes for plants and animals as well as for people. That "global village" for which we rightly hope is not an arrangement for human life alone; it is community of biotic communities.

More specifically, two social values must be actualized in substantial degrees if a "global village" characterized by shalom is to be approximated: justice and sustainability.3 Here the word "justice" refers to three states-of-affairs: economic equity, maximization of opportunities for participation, and a respect for personal liberties. In a global village that is just, people in their respective communities will be free from poverty, unemployment, and hunger; they will be free to participate in the decisions by which their lives are affected; and they will be free to dissent, to choose religions and philosophies of their own, and otherwise to express their individual lifestyle preferences. Of course, sometimes a trade-off is required among these values, but the ideal is for a balance among, and joint approximation of, all three.

The achievement of such balance and approximation need not mean that the world be presided over by a single, world government. A global village can be pluralistic in its cultural and ethnic diversity, and in its political makeup. Indeed, we rightly imagine many governments, with their respective modes of operation, differing according to the dictates of their peoples. But if the global village is to be just, each government in its own way must assure equity, participation, and personal liberty.

The word "sustainability" pertains to the relationship of a just human society to its natural environment. Generally speaking, "sustainable" means sustainable into the indefinite future given the realities of environmental limits. As Charles Birch and John Cobb explain, in a sustainable global village the following characteristics will obtain:

1. The population will be well within the carrying capacity of the planet. What that population would be depends on the economic habits and social organization of the society.
2. The need for food, water, timber, and all other renewable resources will be well within the global capacity to supply them.
3. The rate of emission of pollutants will be well below the capacity of the ecosystem to absorb them.
4. The rate of use of non-renewable resources such as minerals and fossil fuels will not outrun the increase in resources made available through technological innovation.

5. Manufactured goods will be built to last; durability will replace planned obsolescence. Wherever possible materials will be recycled.

6. Social stability requires that there be an equitable distribution of what is in scarce supply and that there be common opportunity to participate in social decisions.

7. The emphasis will be on life, not things; in quality, not quantity; on services, not material goods.[4]

To these seven characteristics of sustainability in relation to nature we must add an eighth: respect for individual animals under human subjugation, e.g. animals in factory farms and scientific laboratories. Such respect may or may not be necessary for our survival into the indefinite future; in any case it is necessary for the animal's own well-being. As we imagine societies that are informed by these eight features of sustainability, and that simultaneously exemplify the three-fold notion of justice previously described, we are imagining the contours of our best hope.[5]

Justice and sustainability, however, while necessary features of the kind of world we hope for, are not themselves sufficient. To these two social values we must add still another: harmony with God. The notion of shalom itself implies harmony, not simply between creatures and creatures, but also between creatures and God. This harmony involves the ethical dimension of life—the dimension of doing God's will by living justly and sustainably—but it also involves more. It involves a love of beauty and a desire for truth as well as the enactment of goodness. To dwell in shalom is to see the presence of the world with an appreciation and empathy that mirrors God's own, to enjoy the gifts of embodied existence, to use one's intellectual and creative talents freely and fully, and to discover God in ways that are sometimes deeply personal and private. Shalom implies a search, and indeed a discovery, of "sacred ground."

This is not to say that justice and sustainability can be separated from harmony with God, or that one can have a harmonious relation with God without living justly and sustainably. One cannot. Rather, it is to say that there is a spiritual or God-related dimension to life and to the very quest for justice and sustainability. As Soelle reminds us, it is the emptiness of a strictly secular approach that moves people beyond the "second phase" of their religious journey toward the third phase: the search for sacred ground. Our best hope is that there can be societies in which people enjoy justice, sustainability, and spiritual harmony.

## The Need for Ecological Thinking

It is one thing to identify our best hope, and another thing to achieve it. We have no assurance that our best hopes, at least for life on this planet, will be realized. The negative scenarios described earlier can well occur. Even tomorrow there could be a nuclear holocaust. Indeed, even today.

Our task, of course, is to do our best to allow the more hopeful future to be realized. None of us, individually or collectively, has the power to "determine" the future. The future unfolds in accordance with factors that are beyond human control, ranging from natural powers to God. Human agency is simply one of many factors that determine the historical future. The best we can do is to try to influence the future in ways we deem healthy, to allow it to unfold in ways that are life-affirming. And to influence it in this way, at least two things are required of us: *right action*, to phrase it in a way that resembles the Eightfold Path of Buddhism, and *right consciousness*.

Right action occurs at two levels. On the one hand, it occurs at the political level. We must act in ways that influence public policies and transform systems of political economy. We do this both within and outside the system. Voting is one way of influencing public policy, but so is nonviolent resistance of the sort espoused by Mohandas Gandhi of India and Bishop Desmond Tutu of South Africa. On the other hand, right action on our part occurs at the level of personal lifestyle. For those of us who are in a position to do so, we must learn to live with less goods so that the limited resources of the globe can be distributed more equably. As the economist E.F. Schumacher put it, "The rich must learn to live more simply so that the poor can simply live."

In the short run, certain forms of coercion, or at least strong incentives, may be required to encourage a simplification of lifestyles on the part of the affluent, global minority. In the long run, however, the only way the rich will learn to live more simply is if they do so out of an inward motivation: that is, out of right consciousness. To speak of right consciousness is not to suggest that there is a single set of doctrines to which all right thinking people need to conform. It is good that there are many different religious and philosophical points of view. But it is to say that there is a very general habit of thought and feeling, characteristic of rich and poor alike in today's world, which must indeed be transcended if the world is to progress toward a more shalom-filled existence. This habit of thought is rightly identified by numerous thinkers in different parts of the world as the "mechanistic" perspective, and increasingly it is compared with a more relational way of thinking which I will call an "ecological" point of view.

In the latter decades of the twentieth-century, several promising versions of ecological thinking are being developed. These include the perspective of "deep ecology" developed by the Norwegian philosopher Arne Naess and the North American thinkers such as George Sessions and Bill Devall; the visionary work of Catholic "geologian" Thomas Berry; liberation theologies developed in Latin America, Asia, Africa, and North America; feminist points of view developed by thinkers such as Rosemary Radford Ruether and Mary Daly; a science-based ecology such as that developed by the physicist David Bohm; the ecological philosophy of Martin Heidegger; the Buddhist ecological visions of Japanese thinkers such as Kitaro Nishida and Keiji Nishitani; the Hindu ecological vision of Sri Aurobondo; contemporary statements of prehistoric and primal (e.g. Native American and African) ecological perspectives; and the Whiteheadian or "process" ecological perspective developed by Christian theologians such as John B. Cobb, Jr., Marjorie Suchocki, Charles Birch, David Ray Griffin, Catherine Keller, and others.

# Mechanistic versus Ecological Thinking

All of these perspectives stress a continuity of humanity with nature and a relational understanding of human existence. Although I am influenced by each of these ecological perspectives at various points in this work, it is the process orientation, as indicated in the Introduction, that influences me most. In my view it is the most extensively developed ecological orientation to date, although it can well be enriched by other ecological orientations. Let us turn, then, to the process understanding of mechanistic thinking and its alternative, ecological thinking.

In the context of process theology the word "mechanistic" suggests a certain way of looking at the world, a certain vision of reality. It refers to 1) a deterministic worldview in which the behavior of each living being—be it an amoeba or a porpoise—is understood to be utterly determined by physical and chemical influences from its past; 2) a utilitarian worldview in which the value of each and every living being is understood to be purely instrumental to human purposes rather than intrinsic to the animal or plant itself; 3) a devitalized worldview in which the depths of physical matter are thought to be lifeless and inert rather than vital and creative; 4) a reductionistic worldview in which living wholes—the psyches of animals, for example—are understood to be utterly reducible to non-living molecules and atoms; and 5) when joined with religion, a dualistic worldview in which sharp dichotomies are drawn between the spiritual and the material, the supernatural and the natural, the soul and its body, humanity and the rest of nature.

The "ecological" thinking highlighted by process theologians stresses alternative ideas. It emphasizes that 1) present events, occurring within the depths of matter and in the lives of living beings, are the result not only of physical influences from the past but also of creative "decisions" made consciously or uncousciously by the entities themselves; 2) all sentient beings, from amoebas to porpoises, are of intrinsic value, in and for themselves, even as they are of instrumental importance to others; 3) physical matter itself, even that composing so-called dead matter, is self-creative in its ultimate depths; 4) living wholes, such as an animal psyche, are more than the parts of which they are composed; and 5) reality itself, while multifaceted and diverse, is better characterized as a vast network interdependent and interfusing events than as a dualistic and dichotomized aggregate of mutually-incompatible substances.

Each of the ideas just noted will be further explained in subsequent chapters. At this stage, it is best to focus on one additional way of identifying the difference between mechanistic and ecological thinking. I will focus on mechanistic thinking as *atomistic* and ecological thinking as *relational*.

A mechanistic model involves the assumption that the building blocks of the universe, whether microscopic or macroscopic, are self-contained and radically independent atoms. Here the word "atom" is not used literally to point to microscopic entities within the depths of matter, but rather figuratively to denote a self-enclosed substance of any sort, microscopic or macroscopic. An atom is first and foremost an individual-in-isolation. Only secondarily, if at all, is it an individual-in-community.

Of course, in the twentieth century many natural scientists have abandoned an atomistic way of thinking as defined above. If by "atom" we mean a self-contained and indivisible entity that first exists and then only secondarily enters into relations with others, then many physicists will deny that there are atoms. Quantum mechanics and relativity theory both encourage a quite different and radically less substantialistic understanding of what microscopic atoms are like. Likewise, many biologists have moved beyond atomism in their ways of thinking about living organisms. Ecological studies show that living organisms are what they are in relation to, rather than in independence from, their surrounding environments; and evolutionary theory shows that a given organism is very much dependent on its predecessors in order to be what it is. Much contemporary physics and biology point beyond an atomistic way of thinking toward a more relational perspective, and it is no accident that process theologians have borrowed a word from biology— ecology—in order to point toward that mode of thinking which they deem so important for contemporary Christians.

Despite movements beyond atomism within some quarters of the natural sciences, however, atomistic thinking remains very much alive in the broader international culture. It is particularly present in the attitudes and policies of industrialized and industrializing nations that are influenced by the modern West. For example, an atomistic way of thinking is evident when the human self or psyche is viewed as having its real identity in self-contained isolation from surrounding social and physical realities. The self is seen as the isolated ego of Cartesian philosophy: an ego whose existence many Western philosophers and social scientists in the twentieth century have denied, but which seems to survive in popular religious understandings of the "soul." Indeed, it is the soul which in the minds of many fundamentalist Christians is to be "saved" by God for the pleasures of heaven, while other souls are allegedly condemned by God, or by themselves, to the flames of hell. The fact that in fundamentalistic thinking human destinies can be so sharply distinguished shows just how atomistic these souls are.

## "Them" Against "Us"

In other circles it is not so much the *individual soul* that is viewed atomistically as it is the *group soul*. The result of a group soul mentality is often ethnocentrism, in which the value of a seemingly self-contained and independent "we" is celebrated over against a stereotyped and objectified "they." Particular instances include religious intolerance, in which a "we" who know the right path to salvation are distinguished from a "they" who are ignorant; racial bigotry, in which a "we" who are racially pure are distinguished from a "they" who are racially impure; sexual chauvinism, in which a "we" who are of superior gender are differentiated from a "they" who are not; East-West policy regarding nuclear war, in which a "we" who inhabit one land consider the possibility of winning a nuclear exchange with a "they" who inhabit another land; and class domination, in which a "we" who are economically and politically advantaged either oppress or exercise paternalistic control over a "they" who are poor or oppressed. In each instance the "we" is a collective atom, a group soul, separated from, and celebrated over against, another collective atom called the "they."

Of course, ethnocentrism is not the only problem with we/they thinking. There is also "speciesism," or homocentrism. Here the "we" is humankind as a whole, and the "they" is nonhuman nature. Human life is viewed as apart from, rather than a part of, nature; and nonhuman nature is viewed as having value only in relation to human need. At best, a dualistic perspective of this sort can give rise to an emphasis on conserving nonhuman resources when such conservation is in the interests of human survival; at worst, it gives rise to rampant exploitation. In either instance the value of nature in its own right, apart from its relevance to human existence, is ignored both in thought and practice.[6]

What, then, is the alternative "ecological" perspective? It is a *relational* point of view in which emphasis is placed on the reality of internal relations. One living being is "internally related" to others if the organism's relations to those others are partly constitutive of the organism's own essence. In process theology these relations are not abstract spatial properties such as "above" and "below"; they are, rather, concrete acts of "taking into account" the other entities from the point of view of the entity at issue. Even as living beings have a power for independent creativity and sentience in the present, process thinkers argue, and even as they have intrinsic value as realities for themselves, they are internally related to the past and to the surrounding world. Either consciously or unconsciously they "feel" or "take into account" the past and the surrounding world from a particular experiential perspective, and in so doing they are dependent upon that past and that world. In many respects the specific character of their relations to others are imposed upon them; in some respects they are chosen; but in all respects the relations are part of, rather than apart from, the identities of the entities at issue. Living beings, animals and plants alike, are individuals-in-community rather than individuals-in-isolation.

Relationality also applies in a more general way to communities. A "community" may be an atom, molecule, living cell, animal body, ecosystem, bioregion, or, in its more distinctively human manifestations, a family, neighborhood, town, city, ethnic tradition, or nation. Its members will include human and nonhuman individuals that are voluntarily or involuntarily bound together as mutual participants in one another's destinies. Indeed, the human family is a community of sorts, as is the earth itself and the cosmos as a whole. To say that relationality applies to communities is to say that communities are what they are in relation to other communities, and that, particularly at this stage in history with reference to life on earth, their destinies are interdependent. The web of life is best conceived as a collective "we" in which, ontologically speaking, there are no "theys."

An inclusive appreciation of the web of life leads to a reverence for life. To revere life is to appreciate the value of living beings for themselves, for one another, and for God; and it is to recognize that diverse forms of life contribute to the very wellbeing of God's life. Such reverence need not lead to the view that under *all* circumstances the taking of life, nonhuman or human, is wrong.[7] We must eat in order to live, and in eating we inevitably take the lives of others, even if they are plants rather than animals. As Whitehead put it, "Life is robbery." The direction of ecological thinking such as that proposed in this work is to insist that such robbery occur with discrimination, caution, humility, frugality, and a sense of appreciation for those lives to which, in fact, one's life is intimately indebted. And it is to insist that robbery be minimized as much as possible. As Wendell Berry explains, an ecological orientation approaches life, and even the taking of life, sacramentally.

> To live, we must daily break the body and shed the blood of creation. When we do this knowingly, lovingly, skillfully, reverently, it is a sacrament. When we do it ignorantly, greedily, clumsily, destructively, it is a desecration. In such desecration we condemn ourselves to spiritual and moral loneliness, and others to want.[8]

In light of this sacramental approach to life, ecological Christians rightly act with the intent to maximize the quality, not the quantity, of human life; with a special option for the poor; a minimum impact on wilderness areas and wild creatures; a minimum abuse of individual animals under human subjugation; and a respect for the earth and its life-support systems. Our aim is to allow human *and* nonhuman life to flourish in their intrinsic value.

The emphasis on relationality characteristic of ecological thinking extends also to God. As has often been emphasized in Trinitarian modes of thought, there are internal relations even in the divine life. With its stress on interconnectedness, ecological thinking emphasizes that these relations are not simply a matter of God's relations to Godself; they are also a matter of God's relations to the world. By "world" I mean the earth and its living inhabitants, plus the rest of the cosmos. As events in the world occur, they are taken into account by God, and God's feelings of them are partly constitutive of God's own essence. God "feels the feelings" of living beings, suffering with the sufferings and enjoying with the joys, and in so doing God's own life is affected. God then responds to these events by availing the world of possibilities for wholeness and growth relative to the situations at hand. In human life these possibilities are for justice in times of injustice, for love in times of indifference, for hope in times of despair.

## The Need for an Ecological Spirituality

As important as it may be for us to learn to *think* relationally, it may be even more important that we learn to *feel* relationally. If we are to live in a global village in a manner that is just, sustainable, and spiritually satisfying, we need to learn to feel the presence of other living beings and of the natural world as if they are a part of us. We must feel their presence as if their destinies and our own are intertwined, as if their interests and our own are identified. Stated in biblical terms, we must learn to love our neighbors as ourselves, realizing that our neighbors are part of ourselves.

Ecological feeling is an aspect of what can generally be called "ecological spirituality." By "spirituality" I mean the general style or quality of our experience, as that experience is lived from the inside, and as it is oriented around an ultimate frame of reference or center. Stated another way, a spirituality is how we apprehend the things we experience from a first-person perspective. Our spirituality is not an object we own, nor a process we undergo. Rather, it is the *way* we experience and respond to the data of experience: to other people, to plants and animals, to the earth and sky, to objects of the imagination, and to God. In an ecological spirituality we feel intimately related to these living beings, recognizing that their existence cannot be separated from our own. Our fellow creatures, and God as well, form the inclusive "we" in terms of which we understand our own "I."

Of course, this is a particular understanding of the word "spirituality," and a modern one. In the Middle Ages the word referred to the supernatural as distinct from the material, and to attempts, through prayer and other forms of personal piety, to get one's inner life in touch with the supernatural. It was thought that, through one's spirituality, one could move away from the world toward unity with God, who is apart from the world. Those who engaged in such activities, oftentimes members of the clergy, were thought to be more spiritual than others.

When in the West spirituality has been understood as an act of turning away from the world toward God, it bears the imprint of Neo-Platonism, a Greek way of thinking that influenced Christianity early in its history in the Roman era. Yet spirituality as thus understood bears little resemblance to the Jewish ways of thinking that characterized biblical Christianity, including Pauline Christianity. When Paul speaks of living in the "spirit" of Christ, he does not suggest a mode of existence that is turned away from the world toward God. Rather he suggests a mode that has "put on the mind of Christ," and that therefore sees and loves the world, and indeed the whole world, as God sees and loves it. In many respects Paul's views suggest a more worldly form of spirituality.

Most forms of spirituality have an ultimate focus: an existential center which serves as an object of ultimate concern. This center functions as a frame of reference for understanding other subjects of experience. The anxiety of our age—an age of radical pluralism—is that there are so many centers from which to choose. Our center can be the self, a social group, an abstract ideal, a future possibility, a metaphysical principle, or a divine subject. Capitalism, for example, often invites us to take the self as an ultimate center; classical Marxism invites us to chocse the eschatological possibility of a classless society; Buddhism encourages us to choose the metaphysical principle of "emptiness" or "dependent origination"; and monotheistic traditions such as Judaism, Islam, and Christianity invite us to choose God.

An ecological spirituality that is Christian takes God as the appropriate center of spiritual life. Moreover it takes Jesus Christ, as remembered and interpreted in various strands of the Christian tradition, as a key to understanding God's love. In Jesus, so the ecological Christian claims, we find glimpses of that unbounded love which is characteristic of God's apprehension of the world, and to which, following Jesus, we ourselves strive to be open in our own finite and limited ways. An ecological spirituality seeks to be open to God in our way and our time as Jesus sought to be in his.

Yet an ecological spirituality also assumes that openness to God involves and requires openness to truth, goodness, and beauty wherever they are found. It assumes that Christ lives, not only as the historical Jesus remembered, but also as the universal Logos of the present. To be open to Christ is to be open to the world. Such openness will move beyond the we/they thinking that is characteristic of much of the Christian past, toward that inclusive love which is the Christian ideal. It will be open to other religious and philosophical traditions, both in the sense of affirming their right to exist and in that of learning from their insights, allowing itself to be creatively transformed in the process. Stated simply, an ecological spirituality will be open to, celebrative of, and transformed by, plurality—the sheer diversity of different forms of life, human and nonhuman. It is a Way that excludes no ways.

Let us consider, then, one instance of such non-exclusion, the way in which Christian consciousness can be transformed by an inclusion of insights from Buddhism. This is the task of the next chapter.

## Questions for Reflection and Discussion

1. Of the five scenarios for the future identified in this chapter, which scenario, or which combination of scenarios, seems to you most probable for the year 2020?

2. Review the characteristics of a "just" society and those of a "sustainable" society, and then look at the community and the bioregion in which you live. Which characteristics of justice and sustainability do you see as significantly approximated in your community, and which do you see as seriously lacking? What interest groups in your community are assisting in achieving justice and sustainability? How are churches involved? In your view, have churches been strong advocates for justice or sustainability?

3. Can you imagine a society which is socially just and ecologically sustainable, but not spiritually satisfying? What does "spiritual satisfaction" entail that is not included in justice or sustainability?

4. Review the characteristics of "ecological thinking" and indicate areas in the world today where you see such thinking present.

5. What instances of the we/they dichotomy most deeply shape the thinking of people in your own community? What are the historical origins of these instances? What is happening today in your community to overcome the dichotomy? What role is the church playing?

6. Consider the definition of "spirituality" offered in this chapter. Given this definition, what is the dominant spirituality of the community in which you live? Is it secular or religious? Around what center is it oriented? What kinds of attitudes and approaches to life does it involve? To what extent and in what ways is the dominant spirituality of your community open to ecological ways of thinking?

## CHAPTER Two

# Faith
# Without Absolutes

John was a college student who believed that God was like a rock. Not literally, of course, but metaphorically. He believed that faith in God was holding onto God as tightly as one would hold onto a rock, cleaving to God amid all life's changes. This rock-like God had human-like characteristics. He was as an invisible father who created the world, who intervened from time to time performing miracles, but who for the most part watched what was happening from afar, waiting for the end of time.

This way of thinking worked well until his junior year, when his mother was diagnosed as having terminal cancer. At first he managed to tell himself the pain his mother was experiencing was all for the best, that his rock-like God must be permitting this to happen for reasons beyond his ken. But her pain was so terrible that he couldn't quite believe his own mental gymnastics. The more tightly he held onto God, the more he wondered what this "God" was that he was holding onto. His philosophy courses did not help, because he was learning that many contemporary philosophers simply do not believe in God, and that the whole idea of "absolutes" was called into question by many of our century's most influential thinkers. He began to wonder if "God" was only an idea in his head, and if "faith in God" was not really just an act of "clinging to an idea" even when he had doubts about its truth. The more he tried to dismiss his doubts, the more they plagued him. The more they plagued him, the guiltier he felt for having them. And, the guiltier he felt for having them, the more resentful he felt, even toward God. He became desperate, and he sought help.

He decided to join in group discussions for victims of cancer and their families sponsored by the campus chaplain. There he met an older student, a woman named Maria, who had been invited by the chaplain as a consultant. At an earlier stage in life, Maria had witnessed her own mother's death, and at that time she, like John, had undergone a crisis of faith. Maria seemed to John to be more mature and more wise than he. What she said helped him.

"Each of us must find our own way of imagining God," Maria told him, "but as for me, I don't believe in 'God the rock' any more. If natural images are used, I think of God as more like an invisible river which pervades the whole cosmos, in which all things live and move and have their being. I don't mean that God is not personal; I still pray to God. But I do mean that God, like a river, is not clingable. We can tap into the currents of divine love, and be supported by God, but we cannot hold onto God. If absolutes are things we can hold onto, God is not an absolute."

"I used to think of faith," she continued, "as a kind of clinging to absolutes, but I don't anymore. For me, faith is an act of trusting the unclingable Spirit, of letting go of our absolutes so as to live amid uncertainty and cooperate with the divine currents. Just as when we learn to float in real rivers, we first thrash and flail by trying to grasp the water; so when we first have faith, we thrash and flail by trying to grasp God. But gradually we learn to let go, to float. As an act of trusting God, faith is more like floating than grabbing."

Then she spoke directly to his pain. "Painful as tragic experiences may be," she said, "they help us to let go to realize that God is not an object among objects to hold onto. And when we learn to float—that is, to live in faith—we no longer picture God as an all-powerful, all-controlling power. God does not and cannot prevent all tragedies, but the waters of the Spirit can heal us, particularly if we let go of our humanly-designed absolutes and cooperate with the Spirit's rhythms. I was healed by the waters of the Spirit, John, and I know you can be, too. I think you are experiencing the birth pangs of a new kind of faith."

The subject of this chapter is this new kind of faith: a faith without absolutes. This kind of faith is important to an ecological spirituality for two reasons. First, it can help those of us who try to embody an ecological spirituality to relativize our own perspectives, lest we lapse into a dogmatism of our own. Second, it can open us to an indwelling Spirit who calls us to realize our own capacities for love, for radical openness to the earth, sky, gods, and mortals. A faith without absolutes is a faith that accepts uncertainty, that tolerates ambiguity, and that internalizes, in a finite way, the unlimited love of the divine Mystery. It is the faith of one like Maria, one who is, to use the phrase introduced in the Introduction, a "third-phase Christian."

There may be many versions of such a faith. In keeping with the view that an ecological spirituality, even if Christian, must be open to insights from other religious traditions, the version I propose is heavily influenced by Buddhism. Of all the world religions and philosophies, it is from Buddhism, I believe, that Christians have the most to learn about the fluid nature of reality. Buddhists have seen that human fulfillment, shalom, lies not simply in obtaining things we desire, but in being able to let go of the illusion that things last forever. Challenged by Buddhism, ecological Christians can learn to let go, even of God, so as to allow divine fluidity to flow through our lives.

My version, as mentioned before, is also influenced by process theology, a way of thinking about God which helps us to recognize change even in God, to see that God is an expression of the ultimate fluidity to which Buddhism points, rather than an exception to it. We further see that even God is ecological in a profound sense, that God's body is the universe itself, and that what happens in the universe happens in God. This means that the joys and sufferings of living beings on earth are shared by God, that God is truly "with us," and with all other living beings as well. In an ecological spirituality, so I suggest, faith is not trust in a rigid ground of being; it is, rather, trust in an ever-adaptive lure for becoming, an ungraspable Spirit within the depths of each and every life.

Before turning to Buddhism and to process theology, a further word is in order about why, after all, a faith without absolutes is needed in our time, and about what, after all, an "absolute" is.

## Why a Faith Without Absolutes?

The need for a new kind of faith springs from many quarters. In part it arises out of the pain we sometimes inflict on ourselves when we suppress honest doubts concerning God and the claims of Christianity. Like John, many of us suffer the consequences of pretending that we are certain when in fact we are not. Psychologically, the pretense of certainty is a difficult burden to bear, especially when bought at the price of suppressing legitimate questions and openness to others. We need a faith, and a way of understanding God's presence in our lives, that allows us to doubt, and that sees doubt as an integral ingredient in the healthy faith journey. We need a faith that allows us to doubt even the existence of God.

But it is not only for ourselves that a faith without absolutes may be needed. We also see the need for such a faith when we recognize how often religious appeals to absolutes issue into prejudices against those who do not share our beliefs. Prejudices are usually justified by appeals to ultimate, undoubtable criteria, to conceptual absolutes. Given the predominance of such appeals in churches, we ought not be surprised by what David Shields tells us in *Growing Beyond Prejudices*: According to several sociological studies, "those who attend church are more prej-

udiced than the non-religious person."[1] Nor ought we be surprised, as Holmes Rolston, Jr., suggests, that such prejudices
may extend even to other living beings and the planet earth:
"Surveys indicate that, on statistical average, those who do not
attend religious services value nature more highly than those
who do."[2] Absolutist faith seems to oppress other people and
even the earth itself.

The good news is that there is an alternative, a religious alternative. According to Shields, while studies show that religious
people who appeal to absolutes tend to be more prejudiced than
others, studies also show that highly committed persons "who
see religion as an open-ended process of pursuing ultimate
questions" are "significantly less prejudiced than the average
person."[3] A faith without absolutes is a faith that sees religion as
an open-ended process. Indeed, it is a faith which is itself in process, ever adapting to the inner beckoning of a divine Spirit in
process. Though we rightly name this Spirit "God," we also
rightly recognize, with Maria, that God is not an "absolute."

## Absolute as a Changeless, Graspable Object

But what, after all, is an absolute? In speaking of a faith *without*
absolutes, I use the word "absolute" to refer to a changeless,
graspable object. In a Christian context, two kinds of realities
can be approached as an absolute in this sense: God, and our beliefs and attitudes concerning God.

To illustrate, let us return to Maria's analogy. Imagine a
man—John, for example—trying both to float in a river and to
conceive the river in which he is trying to float. As he tries to
float, he conceives the river by imagining a map of it in his
mind's eye. The river represents God, and his internal map represents his beliefs and attitudes concerning God. He can approach either the river, or his beliefs and convictions concerning
the river, as a changeless absolute. Or he can approach both as
changeless absolutes.

If he approaches the river as an absolute, he tries to grasp it as
something solid, as something he can hold onto. Such grasping

will make it very difficult to float, but he can try nonetheless. In so doing, he makes God a fixed object, an idol, and commits what we might call "God-olatry." Only when he lets go, even of the divine absolute, can he float, supported by the river and guided by its currents. He must let go of God in order to find God, and to let God be God.

If he approaches his internal map of the river as an absolute, he approaches it as something of which he is absolutely certain, almost as if it were an infallible revelation, the perfect "Word of God." He is absolutely certain of its adequacy; nothing can happen which forces him to change it. In this way his own beliefs become a solid object for him, an idol. He commits what we might call "belief-olatry." Only when he realizes that his map has practical value, that it can be modified or even refuted by his experience of the river itself, can he appropriately let the map function as a guide rather than as an authority.

This does not mean that an ecological spirituality will relinquish beliefs. We need maps to guide us in our daily activities, maps that give us the confidence to trust the living waters of Spirit. We need maps of God, ways of thinking about God. The very notion that "God is like a river" is itself a map among maps, offered in part to elicit a deep-seated, ecological faith.

But a faith without absolutes will recognize that no maps—not even process maps—are absolute. We can be freed from absolutizing our theological maps if we recognize that they are partly products of historical conditioning and social contexts; that they are not perfect mirrors of the divine Mystery; that they may conceal as much about God as they reveal; and that, meaningful as they are to us, they may well be false. To embody a faith without absolutes is to take responsibility for the beliefs we choose, to realize that they are fallible, to be willing to modify them when they appear faulty, and to realize that, even if certain beliefs seem provisionally valid, no certainty is possible with respect to their ultimate validity. It is to realize, in the words of Alfred North Whitehead, that "the merest hint of dogmatic certainty as to finality of statement is an exhibition of folly."[4]

## Absolute as an Object of Trust

Of course, there are other meanings to the word "absolute" besides something utterly changeless to which one clings. Sometimes the word "absolute" can refer to a mystery in which we place our deepest trust. Understood in this way, the God to whom an ecological spirituality points is indeed an absolute, but an absolute of a unique sort. God is an absolute whose very nature prevents absolutization.

To "absolutize" something is to render something absolute in the sense of a fixed and changeless object. It is to make something a mental object, a concept, onto which one clings with complete certainty. If, as I suggest shortly, the divine Life is more like a river than a rock, then God cannot be absolutized in this way. With this Life's fluid and adaptive nature, we cannot cling to it, we can only open ourselves to its currents. And with its intangibility, we cannot objectify it in terms of ideas of which we are certain; we can only trust it to support us, realizing that our images of it—including the image of the river—are but metaphors, like fingers pointing to the moon. It is this kind of faith—trust in a Mystery that cannot itself be absolutized—that appropriately nourishes an ecological spirituality.

Such trust will need some beliefs concerning the Mystery, some map of God, however fallible and finite, to orient it. It will need this map, not to use as a crutch by which to hide from honest doubts, or as a sledge hammer by which to beat others over the head, but rather as a guide for swimming, a guide that gives confidence that, after all, if we let go we can float. In what follows I will develop such a map, showing how it is possible to believe that the Mystery is more like a river than a rock and that, for that matter, all actualities of any sort are rivers as well. Here an ecological spirituality, even if Christian, has much to learn from Buddhism.

## Learning from Buddhism

In many ways a faith without absolutes represents a return to the dynamic God of the Bible, a God who is not an object, but a subject, by whom even the faithful can be continually surprised. Sometimes, however, we must venture to other faiths in order to discover the insights of our own religious traditions. My own appreciation of the dynamic nature of the biblical God has been enriched through a dialogue with Buddhism, a religion which, in many of its expressions, is devoid of both God and absolutes. Perhaps my own story at this point can further illustrate the nature of a faith without absolutes.

For some years I have been involved in the Buddhist-Christian dialogue. Heretofore in the history of Christianity, Buddhists have been most visible to Asian Christians, themselves a minority in Asian lands. Asian theologians generally find a dialogue with Buddhism both necessary and valuable for their own reflections on Christian faith. Aloysius Pieris, a Jesuit theologian from Sri Lanka, speaks for many Asian theologians when he claims that Christian theology must be "baptized by immersion" in the waters of Asian spirituality for its own renewal.[5]

Today, however, many non-Asian theologians, too, are in dialogue with Buddhists. Small but growing numbers of Christian theologians in Europe and North America have begun to meet regularly with Buddhists to foster mutual understanding and growth, one result of which is the International Society for Buddhist-Christian Studies.[6] In addition, following the lead of the late American Trappist monk Thomas Merton, many Roman Catholic monastics have begun to use Buddhist meditative practices as an adjunct to their own spiritual disciplines.

Though there have been many Christians over history who are quite free from dogmatism, Thomas Merton was the Christian who most helped me. I admired him as much for what he struggled to be as for what he was. He was, or at least later in his life struggled to be, one of the freest Christians I had encountered. An example of his freedom—a freedom toward which he, too, seems to have struggled—lay in his interest in, and maturing approach to, Buddhism. He seemed free to say, as a Christian, that Buddhists might have something important to say to

Christians. This was my first encounter with Buddhism: an encounter with Buddhism through the eyes of a Zen Catholic.

## No Ground

Thomas Merton was instrumental in demonstrating for many Christians that in Zen, and in many other forms of Buddhism as well, there is simply no ground, no changeless absolute, nothing permanent to which to cling. Reality itself is understood as an interconnected network of interdependent realities with nothing supporting it, at least with no changeless absolute supporting it.

Stated another way, reality is a verb rather than a noun, a flux rather than a stasis, a process of becoming rather than a state of being. Every living being is like a sunrise or sunset whose beauty can only be appreciated amid its transience. Zen is the art of living in the here-and-now, without clinging, but with creativity and a sense of wonder.

It is noteworthy that some of our century's most creative scientists point us toward a similar view of reality. The speculative physicist David Bohm, for example, proposes that all the particles in the universe are instances of a seamless web of becoming, a cosmic "holomovement." Submicroscopic particles are themselves really processes, in each of which every other process in the universe is implicated. The biologist Charles Birch indicates the same about living beings. Living organisms are composed of "events" rather than "things," and each event is what it is by virtue of its dependence on other events. Physical chemist Ilya Prigogine speaks of reality as a creative processes of self-organizing processes, processes that are themselves better understood as verbs than as nouns. Although not all scientists are as verb-centered as these, the dominant trend in science seems to involve a shift from a philosophy of being to a philosophy of becoming. In the frontiers of science, as in Buddhism, solid things are understood to be products of dynamic processes and expressions of such processes. Verbs precede, and give rise to, nouns.

What if the Buddhists and scientists are right? What if the

building blocks of reality are not blocks as all, but rather processes, and the ultimate reality itself is not something solid and
unchanging, but rather a "holomovement" consisting of myriad
sub-movements? Can this way of thinking, this way of understanding ourselves and our world, be reconciled with Christian
faith?

If faith is clinging to a changeless God or to changeless beliefs,
then it cannot. God will be the one, inexplicable exception to the
ultimacy of becoming. And inasmuch as we cling to this exception, we will not be realizing the depth and universality of that
ultimate reality. The Buddhist will sense, and perhaps the scientist as well, that there is one final reality of which we must let go.

But what if faith is not clinging in this way? What if, as I suggest in this work, it is an act of trust, of letting go? This is the
possibility toward which my own encounter with Zen has pointed me, and toward which I think it can point others interested in
an ecological spirituality. The possibility is that 1) Buddhists are
right; reality through and through is a verb rather than a noun;
and 2) God is a Verb among the verbs, indeed the ultimate Verb
in whose life all other verbs live and move and have their being.
It is in affirming this possibility that process theology becomes
so helpful.

## A Process Understanding of God

The way of thinking about God encouraged in process theology
is like that of Maria, the woman who advised John, in the story
that introduces this chapter. Just as fish live and move and have
their being in rivers, so the cosmos, from a process point of
view, lives and moves and has its being in God. In this life, each
being is loved for its own sake and for what it contributes to others. Thus the divine life, the Mystery, is not simply a mind
through which the cosmos receives its order, or a self by whom
the cosmos is beheld; it is a heart.

Two questions often arise when people are introduced to the
process perspective. First, why think the mystery has a heart?
Why speak of the Mystery as a cosmic "thou" rather than an "it";

a consciousness rather than a blind force; a "who" rather than a "what."

Process theology is not limited to "thou" language; indeed, it opens the door for conceiving the Mystery as an it as well as a thou. It can be as appropriate to speak of the mystery as a "cosmic river" or "divine eros" as it can a "divine Father" or "holy Mother." In order to avoid an absolutization of any given metaphors, an ecological spirituality can well follow suit. We rightly shift from one metaphor to another in order to avoid idolatry of any given metaphor. Still, at least from a process perspective, personal metaphors *can* be appropriate. The question is: Why?

Process theologians think of personal metaphors as appropriate because they believe that consciousness—or at least something like it—is the very essence of actuality, be it material or immaterial. As I discuss in Chapter Four, even the so-called dead matter of rocks and stars is imbued with some degree of internal aliveness, some degree of inner, self-moving spontaneity. If God is in any sense actual, then God, too, must be imbued with such aliveness. The Mystery must have awareness of one sort or another. It can be conceived as the ultimate expression of subjective aliveness rather than the ultimate exception to it. For this reason among others, we can speak of the divine Mystery as a thou: as a "Father who art in heaven" or a "Mother who art in our hearts."

But here the second question emerges. Why conceive the Mystery as a *loving* consciousness? Why not see it instead as a callous consciousness who is indifferent to life, or perhaps even as a cruel consciousness who desires the extinction of life? This is where process theologians reveal their Christian orientation. In seeing the Mystery as all-loving, they are influenced by the idea, transmitted through doctrines, rituals, and the communities, that Jesus was, or strove to be, fully loving, and that to the extent he realized this ideal, he revealed God's nature. This means that if we take the love that Jesus strove to embody; if we imaginatively amplify its breadth and depth beyond limit; and if we then envision that breadth and depth as characteristic of a universal, omnipresent consciousness in whom the universe lives, we have an image of God. Whatever else the Mystery is, it is a well-spring of unlimited love.

## Unlimited Love as Inclusive of All Creatures

Unlimited love has at least two characteristics, both of which are important to an ecological spirituality. First, it is universal in scope, inclusive of all creatures toward whom love can be directed. This means that it extends to amoebas, rattlesnakes, and dolphins as well as to humans. Indeed, it extends to other planets and whatever life might exist on them, and to stars, galaxies, and black holes.

Second, it is infinitely tender, desirous of the well-being of each sentient being for its own sake, and cognizant of each being as an end in itself. This means that the divine Mystery is on the side of each and every living being in its struggle to survive, the rabbit as well as the fox. Some living beings may add more to the divine experience than others, but all add something, and none are loved more by God. Thus, amid predator-prey relations, the Mystery is a lure within each for survival and for a unique form of wholeness. God is on the side of the fox and on the side of the rabbit. Should the rabbit escape the fox, God shares in the rabbit's joy and the fox's hunger. By virtue of infinite tenderness, there is suffering even in God.

Why are these two forms of love important? Because each without the other is insufficient for that unlimited love that we imagine of God. Were the love only universal without being tender, it would be like a person who loves "humankind" but who is insensitive to individual humans. It would be wide but not deep, inclusive but not empathetic. On the other hand, were it tender with respect to a few select creatures, human beings, for example, but exclusive of other creatures, it would be like a parent who loves some of her offspring, but not all. It would be deep but not wide, empathetic but narrow. A perfect and therefore unlimited love would be one that is both wide and deep, universalized and particularized, all-inclusive and omni-empathetic. Those who follow an ecological spirituality, I suggest, can believe in the Mystery as loving in just this inclusive sense.

To do so, however, is not to claim with certainty that the Mystery is all-loving. It is not even to claim with certainty that the Mystery has consciousness, or that the Mystery is real at all! A faith without absolutes will remain open to the possibility that, given enough evidence to the contrary, its own trust in a "cosmic river" is misguided. Prompted by the story of Jesus, a faith without absolutes trusts in an all-loving God, and it lives out of this trust. But it recognizes that no human perspective—not even one that speaks of a trustworthy God—is absolute.

Nor does belief in an all-loving God necessarily require, as its complement, belief in an all-powerful mystery. In order to make sense of the many tragedies that life presents, I believe we must reject the view that God "chooses" to permit evil when God could choose otherwise. Of course, this is controversial, and not all who adhere to an ecological spirituality would hold this position. But there seems to me to be simply too much tragedy to absolve God of responsibility if, in fact, God is all-powerful. Not only is there the tragedy that humans inflict upon humans, there is the tragedy that nature inflicts upon humans, and that nature inflicts upon itself. In a faith without absolutes, we rightly trust that God is all-redemptive, that whatever crosses we or others bear, there is still hope for redemption. But our faith is ultimately in a God who resurrects us from crosses, not in a God who prevents crosses. In order to make sense of this, let us return to Buddhism and see how, as process theologians understand it, Buddhists are right: the ultimate reality is emptiness rather than God.

## "No-thing-ness" as the Ultimate Reality

As Thomas Merton and my own experience of Zen suggest, Buddhism provides a resource for Christians, not because in it we find a religion that is so similar to our own, but rather because in it we find a religion that is so different. Whereas the general thrust of traditional Christianity has emphasized an attitude of clinging to a personal God, the general thrust of Buddhism has emphasized liberation from clinging, including cling-

ing to divine beings. Even nirvana, so the Buddhist insists, is not
an object to which to cling, or even a subject that does the clinging. Nirvana is a way of living amid the realization that there
are no substances, no immutable and independent realities to
which to cling, and no subject that does the clinging.

To say that there are no substances to which to cling is not say
that the public world of rocks and trees, or the private world of
thoughts and feelings, is mere illusion. It is to say, however, that
rocks, trees, thoughts, and feelings are part of a beginningless
and endless process of interrelated events: a cosmic story that is
empty of being and yet full of becoming, empty of foundations
and yet full of connections. This cosmic process is that which is
ultimately real. It is the universe itself, understood to be an infinite series of cosmic epochs reaching back into a beginningless
past and extending into an endless future.

This way of thinking is not incompatible with modern science. Consider the big bang theory. It postulates that the universe emerged from a dense ball of energy, from which issued
an explosion yielding the expanding universe of which we are a
part. According to one version of this theory, there will come a
time when this expanding universe begins to contract, devolv-
ing into another dense ball of energy. Buddhists would propose
that the latter dense ball would eventually explode to create another expanding universe, which would then devolve to create
another dense ball of energy, *ad infinitum*. And they would propose that the dense ball of energy that gave rise to our cosmic
epoch was itself the result of a previous contraction of an expanding universe. Thus the history of the universe would be a
beginningless and endless series of explosions, expansions, and
contractions. Buddhists would insist that each event in the series—the reader reading this page, for example—is ultimately
connected to every other event. This vast, intricate web of existence, without beginning and without end, is part of what Buddhists mean by emptiness.[7]

Even as Buddhists emphasize that all events are connected
with each other, they also emphasize that events contain a kernel of creativity, a spark of freedom, by which the moment de-

cides how the influences from other actualities will be appropriated. As you read this page, for example, you are undoubtedly influenced by your body, by things you have read in the past, by your immediate surroundings, by your mood, and by a host of other things. Ultimately, these influences trace back to the beginningless past of the universe. Still, in the present, you are making decisions about whether you agree or disagree with what is being said. Even if we knew all the initial conditions which affect the decision, we could not predict it with absolute certainty. You might say "yes" to these ideas; you might say "no"; you might say "maybe"; or you might say "I don't know." This momentary decision represents that kernel of creativity within the present event, a kernel of creativity which is part of your very existence here and now. You are, in a way, creating yourself at each moment by appropriating all the influences that currently shape you.

Zen Buddhists would further insist that the "you" who is creating yourself is not different from the creating itself. It is not as if you are one thing and your present experience of internally responding to these words another. Rather you are the experience; you are the event here and now. And this creativity in the here-and-now, too, is part of what they mean by emptiness. In Zen-influenced Buddhist philosophies, emptiness refers, not only to the fluidity of reality and the interconnectedness of all events, but also to the self-creativity within each moment. To say that ultimate reality is emptiness, then, is to say that 1) ultimate reality is a beginningless and endless process pure becoming; 2) all events in this process, all instances of this pure becoming, are interdependent; and 3) within the interdependence, each event contains some degree of self-creativity, by virtue of which the future, even of the universe, cannot be predicted with absolute certainty. If we returned to the initial conditions of our big bang, a different evolutionary story might emerge, given the unpredictable creativity inherent in each event. And if the universe is itself a beginingless and endless series of big bangs, the cosmic epochs that ensue from each might themselves be radically different, depending on the "decisions" ingredient in matter itself.

By virtue of the creativity in emptiness, the future is open rather than closed.

The suggestion that ultimate reality is emptiness—and hence that ultimate reality is "empty" of qualities that make it clingable—can sound quite negative. Indeed, there is a negative aspect to it. But there is also a positive aspect. Negatively, it means that there are no "things," divine or otherwise, to be grasped. There are no objects to be permanently owned. Positively, it means that reality is full of actualities-in-process. Reality is a dynamic no-thing-ness, an emptiness in which all beings are becomings.

This is what is meant when a Zen master teaches: "The ultimate reality is emptiness." Neither the world of rocks and trees, hills and rivers, nor the realm of freedom, is being denied. What is meant is that this world to be seen and felt in a new way, under the auspices of pure, self-creative becoming. To the extent that the Christian internalizes this Buddhist insight, then, the Christian is freed from clinging to immutable grounds, including clinging to God as a ground. This insight can contribute to the inner ethos of an ecological spirituality. Ecological Christians, too, can think of God as pure becoming, as no-thing-ness, as a beginningless and endless process of self-creative emptiness.

## God as an Expression of Emptiness

How can we think of God in relation to emptiness? Immediately two options emerge.

The first is to revise the very meaning of the word "God" so that it refers to emptiness itself. In this instance God would be identified with that beginningless and endless process of interrelated events, in itself containing both good and evil, of which all actualities are expressions. God would be identified, for example, with Francis of Assisi as he feeds the birds and with the Nazi Storm Trooper as he murders the Jew. Stated simply, God would be everything that happens as it happens: becoming itself.

The problem for the Christian with this first option is that it denies the purposeful and caring nature of divine existence. It denies that the Mystery is Jesus-like. The God who is emptiness is not a being who calls toward justice, sustainability, and spiritual satisfaction. Indeed, this God is not a being at all. This God is no-thing-ness itself, exemplified anywhere and everywhere as the sheer becoming of what becomes.

A second option is to recognize that God and emptiness are not exactly identical, and then to try thinking of God as a particular form or expression of emptiness, albeit the supreme form. This is to envision God in a more biblical manner: as a being among beings, continually aware of and responsive to events as they occur, availing the universe of possibilities for order and novelty, and availing living beings on earth of possibilities for wholeness at an individual and social level, relative to the circumstance. As one who avails the universe of possibilities for order and novelty, God would work with the self-creativity of the universe, and God would be an instance of that self-creativity. Creatively, God would assist the universe in creating itself. To say that God is "the Creator" would be to say that God is a guide in the evolutionary process, helping to bring order out of chaos. As one who avails living beings on earth of possibilities for wholeness at an individual and social level, God again would work with creaturely freedom. Here God could be envisioned as "the Sustainer" and "the Redeemer" of life on earth. In both roles God would be a being among beings, albeit the supreme being.

Of course, to say that God is a being among beings is not to say that God is located in a particular region of space or has temporal beginning and end. God can well be envisioned as coextensive with the beginninglessness and endlessness of the universe. It is to say, however, that God is *a* reality rather than *ultimate* reality. God would be the supreme instance of actuality-in-process, not the only instance; the supreme instance of interconnectedness, not the only instance; the supreme instance of self-creativity, not the only instance.

This is what process theology suggests. Drawing as it does from the philosophy of Alfred North Whitehead as well as from biblical perspectives, process thinkers in dialogue with Buddhism suggest that God and emptiness are real and yet different.[8] In the words of John Cobb: "The direction is to accept with-

out hesitation or embarrassment the distinction between ultimate reality and God, and to recognize that the God of the Bible
. . . is a manifestation of ultimate reality—not the name of that
reality."[9]

At first glance, the idea that there is a difference between ultimate reality and God can seem to challenge the sovereignty of
God. And indeed, if by sovereignty one means omnipotence in
the classical sense, the process perspective does in fact challenge
sovereignty. To say the God is not ultimate reality is to say,
among other things, that worldly actualities embody a power of
becoming, a creativity, that transcends even God. If by sovereignty, however, one means "omnibenevolence" rather than
omnipotence, then God is in fact sovereign from the process perspective. God is that reality by virtue of which the world is, or
can be, drawn toward fulfillment, its own realization of its deepest potential. Thus God is a being around whom ultimate concern and hope can rightly be oriented, even as one is awakened
to emptiness. As the supreme actuality-in-process, God, not
emptiness, is the appropriate subject of faith.

## The Universe as the Body of God

In some forms of Christianity it has been thought that the only
appropriate subject of faith is a reality that is utterly independent of the world. In an ecological spirituality, by contrast, the
only appropriate subject of faith is one who is profoundly connected to the world, so connected that the ongoing stories of cosmic evolution and biological evolution are part of the Mystery's
very story. In order to understand this, consider three ways of
conceiving God: supernaturalism, pantheism, and the process
option of "panentheism."

From the perspective of supernaturalism, God and the universe are mutually exclusive. God is not a part of the universe,
and the universe is not part of God. The universe, itself created
out of nothing by an act of divine will, is absolutely dependent
on God in every respect. God knows the past, present, and future
of the universe in a single, all-knowing glance, and nothing hap-

pens in the universe that is not permitted by God. God is all-powerful, analogous to a mighty king who rules over his subjects.

Pantheism is almost the exact opposite of supernaturalism. Here God and the universe are precisely identical. God is the totality of all finite matter comprising the universe: nothing more and nothing less. Thus understood, God is not a personal agent who has thought, feelings, or a will; rather God consists of stars and trees, rivers and rocks, the actions of humans and those of all other living beings. If, as Buddhists say, the totality of finite matter is a beginningless and endless process of events-in-transition, then a pantheist would say God is emptiness.

Panentheism is a synthesis of the insights of pantheism and supernaturalism. Literally, the word means everything (*pan*) is in (*en*) the divine (*theos*). From a pan*en*theistic perspective, the universe is, in an important way, a part of God, as pantheism says, but God is also more than the universe, as supernaturalism contends.

The key, however, is to understand how the universe is "part of" God. One option is to see the universe as a manifestation of God's own essence, much as photons are expressions of the sun's substance, or waves are expressions of the ocean's substance. This is the point of view I would adopt if I claim that God is Being Itself, the ground of being. I would conceive the universe as God's emanation.

This is not the way process theology sees it. Process theologians see the universe as "part of" God in the same sense that bodily happenings—pleasures for our palates, for example, or pains in our stomach—are part of our psychic life. Just as what happens in and to our bodies happens in and to us, so process theologians say, what happens in and to the universe happens in and to God. The joys and sufferings of the world are the joys and sufferings of God. Yet just as we, as psyches, are more than our bodily happenings, so God is more than the happenings of the universe. God is also one who responds, as a distinct agent, to the joys and sufferings of living beings. The universe is God's body, and God is more than the universe.

This is not to say that God has a body among bodies, that God can be located somewhere in the heavens. For process theologians as for most Christians, God is everywhere at once. The closest thing God has to a body is the universe itself. Earth and its creatures, plus the heavens and their celestial bodies, are present to God more directly than they are present to us. Almost literally, the world *is* God's body.

Is the power of worldly beings an emanation of divine creativity? From a process perspective, no. Beings in the universe—from quarks within the depths of atoms to human beings—have a creative power of their own which does not come from God and which is itself an instance of that emptiness Buddhists speak of. If a "ground of being" is a source of all the power in the universe, God is not a ground of being. God is, rather, as I shall attempt to illustrate, a "lure," a beckoning presence that leads us to the full expression of our lives as persons.

## A Woman of Faith

What is it like, then, to believe in a God who, though not an ontological foundation, is nevertheless the object—or, better, the living subject—of faith? How do we experience this God? How is this God present in our lives? Consider the faith of Maria, the woman we described earlier, the one who helped John move beyond his faith in a rock-like God.

Imagine that Maria herself embodies an ecological spirituality. This would mean that she lives and acts out of a hope that our world can become much more socially just and ecologically sustainable. Outwardly, she might live this hope by reducing her own consumption of water, energy, and food in order to embody a lifestyle that all could share; by joining an environmental organization which helps to protect the environment; by voting for legislators who promise to help the poor, protect the environment, and respect the rights of animals in laboratories and factory farms; by volunteering her time at a battered women's center or a kitchen for the homeless; or by doing several related activities. Her spirituality, however, would not be exactly identical with these actions. Rather, it would be her way of experiencing, her way of feeling the presence of the world around her and within her, her way of feeling the presence of God.

And how exactly would she feel the presence of God? There are many ways. She could feel the presence of God in nature: in the intricacy of the dragonfly's wing, the awesome power of the ocean, the warmth of the sun, the shimmering luminescence of the moon.

She might also feel the presence of God in prayer, in the sense that there is "someone listening" as she asks for guidance, and in the sense that this someone is also deep within her, in the silent recesses of her own heart.

But how would she experience God in the act of faith, particularly in her faith without absolutes? When she lets go and trusts in the currents of divine love, in what does she place her faith?

## Faith as Openness to the Divine Lure

The answer is in an inwardly felt "lure" toward the fullness of life for herself and others. This lure is like a white light at the center of her existence: a light to which she may be more or less open, but which is always there. It was present within her before she believed in it, and it would be within her even if she ceased to believe in it. She feels its presence within her as a goal rather than a goad, as a pull from ahead rather than a push from behind, as the call of what "can be" rather than the compulsion of what "has been." It is the presence of unrealized possibilities for the fullness of life, for shalom, which she herself, in her self-creativity, can actualize.

At times Maria gives this divine lure different names. Sometimes she calls it the Self of her self, sometimes the Heart of her heart, sometimes the Eros of her eros, and sometimes the Spirit of her spirit. It is so rich in its life-giving potential that no single name seems appropriate. In any case it is that to which she is open amid her faith without absolutes. Her faith without absolutes is trust in an ever-faithful beckoning presence deep within her heart, by which she feels drawn toward shalom. She touches God in the very act of faith.

Maria feels that this presence is what Christians rightly mean by the Holy Spirit. It is through the indwelling Spirit that God is in her life and, for that matter, in every other life as well. The lure that beckons her to realize her own potential, both individually and socially, is the same beckoning presence within each living being to survive with satisfaction. Even as all living beings are in God as part of God's body, so God is within all living beings as part of their desire to live. Indeed, it could be argued that the Holy Spirit is a "cosmic lure" by which the universe in different epochs has been drawn toward those forms of evolution that are richest in potential. Here Maria agrees with the biblical view that through the Spirit of God all things come into existence.

As a Christian, Maria perceives this indwelling lure as part of Jesus' life as well. When the Bible says that "the Word became flesh" in Jesus, she thinks this means "the Lure of God was enfleshed by Jesus." Jesus was open to the call of God, so aligning himself with it that, at times in his life, "his will" and "the will of the Father" became one. He could speak with the authority of God, forgive in the name of God, and heal with the grace of God.

Maria does not think that she can duplicate Jesus' achievement, which itself depended on the grace of God within him. Nor does she desire to do so. She recognizes that Jesus was called by God to be things and do things that she is not. One Jesus is enough. But she does believe that she is called in her own way to be Jesus-like. This is not to repeat the beliefs of Jesus or to absolutize the cultural forms by which he was himself conditioned. It is not necessarily to die on a cross. But it is to be open to the divine call in her way and her time, as Jesus was in his way and his time. She, too, in her own way, feels called to enflesh the Word. This is how, in faith, she tries to follow Jesus.

To follow Jesus is to be true to her own deepest experience of the divine presence, as that experience is nourished by supportive communities of other men and women who, too, seek to embody an ecological spirituality. To explain further, let me identify seven ways in which Maria and others who share her perspectives experience the divine presence. I believe these are ways that many of us who adopt an ecological spirituality can appropriately embody in our own lives.

## Seven Ways of Experiencing the Inward Call of God

First, and perhaps most obvious to many Christians, Maria experiences the divine presence as an invitation to love. This "lure to love" is not only to love others, it is also to love herself. For a true love of others is impossible without some degree of healthy self-affirmation, healthy self-love. Moreover, the lure to love others is not only a lure to love human others. It is also a lure to love all sentient beings, all beings who struggle to survive with satisfaction. The divine presence within us is a lure to recognize the divine in other beings. It leads us to the realization that other living beings, too, are loved by the God within us.

Second, and again obvious to many Christians, Maria experiences the lure of the divine as a beckoning to forgive and to accept forgiveness. Indeed, she can only love herself inasmuch as she recognizes that even the parts of herself that she cannot accept—her jealousies and resentments, for example—are themselves embraced by the divine Heart. She feels the lure of God as a beckoning to accept the fact that she is embraced by God and hence forgiven by God. Indeed, God, the Mystery itself empowers her to forgive herself, to accept the forgiveness of others, and to forgive others. To her friends she seems remarkably free from jealously and resentment, precisely because she feels accepted amid, not apart from, her personal failings.

Third, and sometimes less obvious to many Christians, Maria experiences the divine as a call to be honest, to be open to truth, whatever its consequences for personal belief. It is for this reason that she chooses not to absolutize her own beliefs, even her belief in God. Trustful as she is that there are divine currents within and around her that support and nourish her, she remains open to the possibility that she is wrong, that she is imposing a false interpretation on her own experience. Thus, in response to the presence of God, she is willing to doubt even God.

For the sake of God, and in response to God, she does not absolutize her ideas of God.

A fourth way she senses the indwelling divine presence is as
a call to realize her own creative potential. Inasmuch as she is
open to the divine beckoning, she is open to her own deepest
potential to bring ideas together in new ways, to dream new
dreams, to participate in the adventure of life and the adventure
of the cosmos. The more open she is to the currents of divine
love within her, the freer she feels to be herself, to let the creative juices flow within her own psyche. She feels beckoned by
God, not to suppress her creativity in obedience to an external
creator, but rather to become, in her own finite and limited way,
a co-creator with God.

A fifth way she experiences the indwelling presence is as a beckoning to appreciate beauty, from the intricate complexities of
molecules and atoms, through the wondrous creations of art
and music, to the awesome attractiveness of the heavens above.
In faith, she senses that this beauty is part of an ultimate beauty,
a divine beauty, which permeates the entire universe. Her faith
without absolutes is a faith in the self-justifying power of beauty, a faith that meaning in life often hinges, not on the acquisi-
tion of happiness, but rather on a participation in beauty.

A sixth way she encounters God is as a call to let go, to accept
change, even change in God. One reason Maria cannot cling to
God is because the possibilities to which she is open in faith are
themselves always changing. When her mother was dying of
cancer, the possibilities she derived from God were for courage;
when she was deciding to return to school, they were for adventure; when she was counseling John, they were for compassion.
That fulfillment toward which she was called at age six was not
the same goal toward which she was called at age twenty-six,
which was still different from that toward which she is called at
age forty-six. Her life is a journey, always beckoned by the One
who is journeying with her and in her. She cannot cling to God,
because God, too, is in process along with her.

A seventh way in which she experiences the unclingable Spirit within her is as a call to be connected, to enter into rich rela-

tions with the rest of God's body. Here, too, her faith has a Buddhist tenor. For if, as Buddhists suggest, all things are profoundly interconnected, then shalom must be, not a denial of this connectedness, but rather an embrace of this connectedness. It is this aspect of the call of God—the call to enter into rich relations with the rest of creation—that serves as a springboard for the rest of this book.

An ecological spirituality begins with a faith of the sort I have described in this chapter. But it does not end there. Through faith an ecological spirituality will feel called to be appreciative of, and connected with, the entire range of existence, which is the depth and complexity of God's body. Earlier I have said that there are four regions comprising this range: the earth, sky, gods, and other mortals. Let us begin with the latter, with mortals, and particularly with other animals. For in the twilight of the twentieth-century, we are in desperate need of reaffirming our kinship with other creatures, of realizing that our own fullness of life cannot be realized apart from a reverence for all life. A faith without absolutes will naturally unfold, among other ways, as an openness to animals.

## Questions for Reflection and Discussion

1. Note the two definitions of "absolute" early in the chapter: 1) a changeless object of clinging and 2) a Mystery in which we place our deepest trust. This chapter proposes that a person can understand God as an absolute in the second sense, all the while denying that God is absolute in the first. In the life of Christian faith as you understand faith, is it actually possible to trust God without making God an absolute in the first sense, or is it the case, contrary to the claims of this chapter, that, in fact, an object of a person's deepest trust must in fact be changeless? In the process of answering this question for yourself, try to define the kinds of "change" which can be admitted in God and the kinds which, from your own point of view, ought not be admitted into our understanding of God.

2. From the point of view of an ecological spirituality, so this chapter suggests, God is all-loving, but not all-powerful, at least if "all-powerful" means capable of preventing all tragedies. From the perspective of a faith without absolutes, things happen in the world that even God cannot prevent. Is such a God worthy of worship? Respect? Trust? Faith? Or is such a God too weak to inspire such responses? From your own point of view, must a God worthy of the name "God" be all-powerful?

3. When a Buddhist says that there is "no ground," what does she mean? What does she mean by "emptiness"? This chapter suggests that those who live an ecological spirituality can assent to these ideas, and internalize them as deeply as possible, all the while continuing to believe in God. From your point of view, is this actually possible? Or must the Christian finally deny that "emptiness" is the ultimate reality?

4. From the perspective of an ecological spirituality, God is unlimitedly loving. This means, among other things, that the cosmic Life loves all living beings for their own sakes: not only those whom we are able to befriend, such as dogs, cats, chimps, and porpoises, but also those that threaten human life, such as the AIDS virus and malarial mosquitoes. Some creatures, those with high degrees of sentience, for example, may add to the life of God in ways others cannot, but none are loved more than others. Is God as thus conceived too loving? Explain your answer.

5. What is the difference between panentheism and pantheism? In what ways is the God to whom panentheism points transcendent, and in what ways not?

6. Which of the seven ways of experiencing the inward call of God seems most important to you, given your own spiritual journey and your own understanding of an ecological spirituality? What ways can and should be added to this list?

## CHAPTER THREE

# Openness
# to Animals

Imagine a dialogue in a Sunday school class between a woman who is active in the animal rights movement and a fellow member of her class. Their church sanctuary is being remodeled, and the class is discussing options for the new building. Suddenly the conversation takes a strange turn.

"Someone needs to create a crucifix," she proposes, "in which a cow is nailed to a cross, legs outstretched like Jesus. And another in which a hog is nailed; and still others in which dogs, cats, chicken, chimps, and rabbits are nailed. And sculptures of this sort ought to be placed in churches and perhaps even on altars, accompanied by other sculptures in which raped women, hungry children, abandoned elderly people, and the earth itself are placed on crosses. This would remind us that Jesus was not the only victim of our inhumanity."

One man in her class is particularly shocked by what he considers her blasphemy. "Jesus was not an animal," he says, "he was God!"

"I know that," she says. "I believe he was God, too; at least if by 'being God' we mean that in him we see God's presence. Through Jesus all of us in this class are invited to trust that God has a heart as well as a mind, an all-compassionate heart. But Jesus *was* a man. He was influenced by his culture as are we; and he had genes and hormones just like we do. Even as one through whom the light of God shone, Jesus was a human among humans, a mammal among mammals, a vertebrate among vertebrates."

The man becomes angry: "But to say he was a mammal is to insult him, to make him beneath us. He may have been a 'man,' but he was not an 'animal.'"

"No, he was an animal," she insists. "There's nothing *wrong* with being an animal. We ourselves are creatures among creatures, animals among animals. Of course we are special animals, because we have capacities for love and wonder that many other animals lack. If we want to use biblical language, we are animals made in the image of God, because we can mirror God's love in ways that most other animals cannot. But these capacities don't make us supernatural beings, they make us creative extensions of the evolutionary process. It is good to be an animal; even Genesis says as much."

The man is not convinced. "But you can't place crucifixes with animals on them alongside Jesus, and you can't place crucifixes with other humans on them either alongside him. That will dilute his importance!"

"Was Jesus insulted by being placed on a cross alongside two other men? Two criminals?" the woman asks. "I don't think so. He identified with the victims of society, the 'least of these.' He said that whoever follows him serves the poor, the outcasts, the neglected. We don't insult Jesus by putting other victims alongside him; we identify with his cause."

"But Jesus didn't identify with other animals," the man insists. "And to extend our love to such animals is to go beyond what we see in Jesus."

"I know it," she says. "Today we are aware of many victims in addition to those for whom he expressed concern. For example, Jesus didn't express explicit concern for a victimized earth, but we know today that the earth is victimized by widespread despoliation, and that it needs our protection. To follow Jesus is not to limit ourselves to the victims he knew in his time; instead it is to take up his cause of identifying with the victims, wherever and whoever they are. Today we see, perhaps more explicitly than Jesus did, that humans are not the only victims in this world. Anything that can feel, that can suffer pain, that has importance to itself, can be a victim. Most of us in this class already know that. That's why we try not to be abusive to animals."

"If we know it," the man says, "why do we need to talk about it, much less put animals on crosses?"

"What many of us don't know," she says, "is that we live in a society that has institutionalized the abuse of animals, just as it has institutionalized racism, poverty, and a victimization of women. We Christians need to wake up to this fact. We need to live lives of reverence for all life, not human life alone. Only then can we truly live up to, and extend, Jesus' hope for shalom."

Then she asks a question of the entire class, one that that seems irrelevant to him.[1] "How many of us washed our faces today; how many brushed our teeth; how many used cologne, perfume, after-shave lotion, mascara. How many of us have used window cleaner or detergent within the past week, or furniture or floor polish within the past month? How about oven cleaner or paint?" Nearly all raised their hands; she as well.

"Let me give an example of what I'm talking about when I speak of institutionalized abuse. What we don't realize is that almost all these cosmetics and household products were first tested on animals in painful ways. I'm talking about things like acute eye-irritancy tests, and tests in which animals are force-fed a deodorant or floor polish until a specific number die. When we purchase these products, we support the pain and death, primarily for the sake of modest comforts. We don't have to harm animals directly to be cruel to them; we can be cruel by supporting others who are cruel. Let me give you just one example."

She goes on to describe an eye-irritancy test, the Draize Test used by many cosmetic manufacturers.[2] "You start with six albino rabbits. You take each animal and check that the eyes are in good condition. Then, holding the animal firmly, you pull the lower lid away from one eyeball so that it forms a small cup. Into this cup you pour 100 milligrams of whatever you want to test. You hold the rabbit's eyes closed for one second and then let it go. In order to keep the rabbit from dislodging the substance in any way, you immobilize the rabbit by keeping it in a holding device where only the head protrudes. You might even keep the rabbit's eyes permanently open by using metal clips. The animal may squeal, try to claw at the eye, jump or escape, but the immobilizing device keeps him still. After several days you come back and see if the lids are swollen, the iris inflamed, the cornea ulcerated, or if the rabbit is blinded in that eye. And all this for helping us to become more vain!"

Those who follow an ecological path need not insist that crosses with animals and other people be placed alongside crucifixes of Jesus in churches. But we can and should recognize that the idea behind such crosses is important. The woman in the animal rights movement exemplifies an important feature of an ecological spirituality: reverence for animals.

Recall that an ecological spirituality is open to the earth, sky, gods, and mortals. Animals are among the mortals to whom ecological Christians are open. Just as the love of God is inclusive of all animals, so an ecological spirituality will be inclusive of animals; and just as the love of God is responsive to each animal for its own sake, so, inasmuch as is possible, an ecological spirituality will be responsive to animals for their own sakes. Of course, the earth supports countless animal species. There is no way we can be responsive to each. Moreover, we cannot and ought not go into the wilderness and save all prey from all predators. Such would wreak havoc on the ecosystems, creating more destruction than wholeness. But we can be responsive to those individual animals whom we have brought into our community, whom we have "domesticated" in our factory farms and scientific laboratories. An ecological spirituality that fails to be concerned for "the least of these" is not sufficiently ecological.

The purpose of this chapter, then, is to describe that part of an ecological spirituality that is open to animals. The chapter is divided into three sections. In the first section, I further articulate the areas of abuse of animals in contemporary society; in the second, I discuss five ways in which an ecological spirituality will incorporate the presence of animals; and, in the third, I discuss what ecological Christians can do to remedy the contemporary abuse of animals.

## The Problem

How are animals abused in contemporary industrial societies? The woman in the Sunday school class mentioned one way: the infliction of pain on animals in testing cosmetics and household products. Perhaps two more illustrations will be instructive.

**Food** Consider, for example, the way animals are raised for food in the United States and other industrial countries. In the United States alone, tens of millions of animals are killed each year to provide meat for human consumption. Like us, they die individually, one-by-one. Most of them are reared indoors in factory-style farms by means of "close-confinement" or "intensive rearing" methods. The animals enjoy no sunlight, no fresh air, and, often, no room to turn around. If they are laying hens, they are sometimes packed in groups of six to eight in wire-mesh metal cages the size of a page of daily newspaper; if they are pigs, they are often confined for up to five years in stalls just larger than their own bodies; if they are veal cows, they are taken from their mothers at birth and raised in permanent, restrained isolation. Confined in these ways, many forms of natural behavior are frustrated, from preening and dust bathing in chickens to nursing and gamboling in veal cows. When their human producers think they are ready, these animals are transported by truck and rail to slaughter, during which many suffer stress, injury, and even death. They are slaughtered in different ways. Chickens are hung upside down on conveyer belts and cut with a knife; pigs and cows are stunned by an electric current or captive-bolt pistol, after which, while unconscious, their throats are cut.

The goal of intensive rearing methods is to raise the maximum number of animals in the minimum amount of time with a minimum investment, so as to make as much money as possible. In the process the animals are treated almost exclusively as means to ends, and never as ends in themselves, much less as creatures loved by God. Intensive rearing methods began to be used with frequency in the years before World War II, when poultry farmers in urban areas discovered that such methods helped them to increase production in order to meet rising demands for eggs and meat. Since that time, factory farms have become the stock-in-trade of agribusiness. In the United States today, almost all poultry products and half the milk and red meat come from large-scale indoor production.

**Fashion**  Or consider fashion in industrial nations. If we of the northern hemisphere are among the affluent minority in the world, most of us know our own tastes in clothing are considerably engineered by fashion designers and large corporations. The fact that we "like" blue jeans or tweed jackets is itself the result of expensive advertising paid for by these groups. What we may not recognize is that many of our clothes, those made of fur or leather, for example, are enjoyed at the cost of animal suffering. Consider furs. As a consultation in 1988 sponsored by the World Council of Churches explains, "Fur-bearing animals trapped in the wild inevitably suffer slow, agonizing deaths, while those raised on 'modern' fur farms live in unnatural con-

ditions that severely limit their ability to move, groom, form social units and engage in other patterns of behavior natural to
their kind."[3] When we purchase the products of commercial fur-
riers, we support the pain and death of these animals. Moreover, we do so unnecessarily, for attractive coats, gloves, capes,
and the like which are not linked with the commercial exploitation of animals exist and are available for consumption. Even
more of these non-exploitable products would be available if
we, the consumers, demanded them.

Food and fashion are only two additional examples of the
abuse of animals. An exhaustive list would include the use and
abuse of animals in experimentation in the natural sciences and
in science education, much of which is unnecessary, wasteful,
and poorly executed; the exploitation of animals in recreation,
including rodeos, cockfights, bullfights, and circuses; the indis-
criminate killing of animals in sport hunting, and the cruel treatment of pets.

The underlying problem, however, is a spiritual problem.
Other animals are treated in these ways because we ourselves
have been conditioned to think of them primarily, if not exclusively, as objects for our use. We have learned to think of them
as means to our ends, as being mere instruments for our well-
being, as having been "given to us" by the Creator. We feel as if
we have a right to treat them in any way we wish.

But do we? From the perspective of an ecological spirituality,
we do not. An ecological spirituality will be sensitive to the fact
that other animals are ends in themselves, and not just means to
our ends. Indeed, from the point of view of one who seeks to revere all life, other animals can be perceived in at least five ways.

## Five Ways of Perceiving Animals

**Animals as Having Intrinsic Value** First, animals can be seen
as having value in and for themselves as well as value for others. Put in more technical terms, they can be seen as having *in-*

*trinsic* as well as *instrumental* value. Another creature has intrinsic value if it is important in its own right and for its own sake. It has instrumental value if, in addition to its importance for its own sake, it has importance for other creatures, if it is useful to them.

In Christianity, it has often been emphasized that human beings alone have intrinsic value, and that the rest of creation has only instrumental value for humans or for God. An ecological spirituality diverges from this traditional Christian perspective. It recognizes that each and every living being has intrinsic value.

Three further points, however, need to be made about intrinsic value. First, life inevitably involves the taking of other life. Every time we wash our faces we kill billions of bacteria; every time we eat, we support the death of plants, and often, animals. Because life is, in a sense, a type of robbery, ecological Christians must inevitably make decisions about whom to rob, when to rob, how to rob, and, most importantly, how to minimize robbery. To make such decisions, it is necessary to distinguish degrees of intrinsic value among different kinds of organisms, albeit with humility and amid honest uncertainty. To distinguish degrees of intrinsic value is to say that some animals may have more "value in and for themselves" than others.

One possible criterion by which we might distinguish degrees of intrinsic value is the capacity of a living organism for richness of experience. Here "richness of experience" refers to both the degree to which an organism can enjoy a wide variety of influences, both bodily and environmental, and to the creativity with which it can respond to more influences. A man in a comatose state, for example, no doubt experiences some richness of experience, albeit less than when he is awake. He has more value in and for himself when awake than when comatose. Similarly, some organisms may have more value in and for themselves than others; they may be able to experience more "richly" than others. The more complex an organism's nervous system, the greater its capacity for richness of experience, the greater its intrinsic value. Herein lies the justification, for example, at least from the point of view of an ecological spirituality, for taking the lives of cancer cells over those of humans.

Herein also lies the justification for preferring to eat plants over animals if at all possible. Plants are best understood as tremendously complex and beautiful colonies of cells. Each cell in a plant may well have a richness of experience of its own, a perspective that is enriched by its associations with other cells in the plant colony and that contributes to the richness of those cells. But, in contrast to animals, plants do not seem to have psyches that receive influences from all the cells and that initiate responses. If we use a metaphor from politics, plants are more like "democracies" without a presiding subject. On the other hand, animals are like "monarchies." In addition to the myriad cells that make up an animal's body, an animal seems to have a psyche, a presiding subject, that feels the influences from the various cells that initiates coordinated responses. Whereas a plant is a body of cells without a presiding subject, an animal is a body of living cells with a presiding subject. If we speak of a "plant's experience," we are really speaking of the myriad experiences enjoyed by the plant's cells; when we speak of an animal's experience, we are speaking of the experiences enjoyed by the animal psyche. Because the animal has, or better is, this psyche, and because this psyche is able to gather and enjoy influences from so many more sources than those available to any given cell in the animal body, the animal has great capacities for richness of experience. Moreover, the animal has greater opportunities for richness of experience than would the plant. If we must take a life, better to take that of a plant than an animal; and if we must take an animal life, it is better to take the life of an animal with a less complex nervous system, and hence a lesser capacity for richness of experience, than to take the life of an animal with a more complex nervous system.

The second point to make, however, is that this measure of an organism's intrinsic value is done as a last resort, not as a first resort. Admittedly, the measure is itself speculative; we do not really know that a cancer cell has less intrinsic value than the person it inhabits, or that a ringworm causing fungus has less intrinsic value than a dog whose skin cells it inhabits, or that a plant has less intrinsic value than does an animal. Those who follow an ecological path will try their best to respect all living beings as having intrinsic value, and then evaluate degrees of intrinsic value only when necessary. The deepest sensitivity of the ecological Christian is that life—all life—has value in and for itself.

The third point to make is that a recognition of an animal's intrinsic value in no way belies the fact that the animal is a relational creature. We humans, for example, are thoroughly relational. Our inner lives emerge as creative responses to our bodies and our surroundings, or, to put it in terms of this work, as creative responses to the earth, sky, gods, and other mortals. The value we have in and for ourselves is a value that emerges out of our relations with others. Similarly, a doe in a forest has intrinsic value, but this value is not an atomized substance that cuts her off from her surroundings. Rather, her intrinsic value is the quality of her experience as that experience itself emerges in response to the food she eats, the things she smells, the goals toward which she is drawn, the internal imagery that appears to her in dreams, the plants and other animals she perceives in her surroundings, and her relations with other deer. In her own way, she, too, is a synthesis of relations to the earth, sky, gods, and other mortals. Her intrinsic value is the subjective side of these relations. In an ecological spirituality, we learn to see other animals as kindred creatures, each a subjective synthesis of relations to the earth, sky, gods, and other mortals.

**Animals as Kindred Creatures Loved by God**   A second way in which we can see other animals, as well as individual cells in plants, is as kindred creatures loved by God. To be loved by God is more than simply having instrumental value to

God; it is more than just contributing to the joy of God, to the richness of the divine consciousness. It is to be a subject of divine care and concern. Just as a parent loves a child for the child's sake, or a lover loves a beloved for the beloved's sake, so in an ecological spirituality, God loves all creatures for their own sakes. Creatures are perceived as God's beloved, as God's children.

This way of seeing is particularly important as a means of offsetting the potential dangers of ranking creatures in accordance with degrees of intrinsic value. For while a cancer cell may have less intrinsic value than the person whose body it inhabits, or a ringworm-causing fungus may have less intrinsic value than the dog it inhabits, both the cancer cell and the fungus are subjects of divine love. They, like the person and the dog, are loved for their own sakes. Moreover, there is something immeasurable about this love. We rightly imagine that God does not love them less than the person and dog, just differently, according to their capacities to receive love.

And how do they receive divine love? The answer is through what in the previous chapter I called "the lure of God." This divine lure is within each creature—cancer cells and fungi as well as dogs and humans—as an indwelling call to seek the fullness of life relative to the situation at hand. In human life we speak of it as a lure to shalom, but an ecological Christian can recognize that other creatures, too, have their own kinds of shalom. God's love is not a disinterested love, it is an omni-interested love. Its interest is in the well-being of each and every living being, which means that, at least in life as we know it, there is tragedy and heartache, even in the divine heart. I believe we rightly imagine that the divine heart hopes most for the survival of those creatures whose capacities for sentience are richest, but we must also recognize that the divine heart hurts when any creature, even the least of these, is frustrated in its will to live.

The recognition that God loves each creature for its own sake also suggests a new twist on the theme of divine praise. In much traditional Christianity, other animals have often been seen as having only instrumental value to God, at best as being creatures who in some way "praise" God along with righteous human beings. An ecological spirituality can add a new insight. It can see that, as a lure within them for survival and satisfaction, God in a way "praises" animals. From the vantage point of an ecological spirituality, Yahweh's pleasure—to use biblical terminology—is not simply that they give him satisfaction; it is also that he is able to give them pleasure. He bestows his blessings on animals as best he can. If by "praise" we mean an expression of approval, then God "praises" animals. To be an ecological Christian is to praise animals as God praises them.

**Animals as Extensions of God's Body**  Third, in an ecological spirituality, other animals will be seen as being parts of God's body, and therein as contributing to the divine life. In this respect they do indeed give God pleasure, even as God lures then toward their own well-being. When animals suffer pain, the pain belongs to God as well; when they experience joy, the joy is God's. As aspects of the divine body, animals and plants are part of the vast tapestry of life which is the divine life. What happens in and to them also happens in and to God. This sensitivity gives an additional reason for wanting to protect domesticated animals with a high degree of sentience from unnecessary abuse. Not only do we do so for their sakes, we also do so for God's sake.

To see animals and plants as parts of God's body is to to recognize that there is movement in God, that the dance of life on earth is a dance in the life of God. The tapestry of life, and indeed the tapestry of the entire creation, is not a fixed tapestry. It is always in motion, ever-changing. So God is always in motion and ever-changing. The divine love is constant and ever-faithful, yet the content of the divine lure for each creature is changing with different circumstances. In the dance of creation, it is not just that God leads, it is that God's partner—the creation itself—also leads, and that God follows.

The divine dancer follows by responding to each new situation with a new opportunity for wholeness relative to the circumstance at hand.

**Animals as Spiritual Guides** A fourth way in which ecological Christians can view animals is as spiritual guides through whom we learn about God. This is the case both with pets and with animals in the wild.

With respect to pets, for example, more than a few dog owners have enjoyed that unconditional love that comes from a faithful dog. If we have treated our dog kindly, we are loved by our dog no matter who we are or what we have done. We do not have to prove ourselves to the dog; the dog simply loves us. Such love is one way we can better understand the unconditional love of God for the whole of creation, including ourselves. An ecological spirituality will be able to discern God in other animals, to see the Mystery in the mystery of another creature's interiority.

Animals in the wild can also be spiritual teachers. We do not often learn from them about divine love, but we do indeed learn about divine otherness. For wilderness itself reminds us that there is more to life than our own human perspective, and more to God than our own humanly-designed conceptions and images of God. Animals in the wild remind us that there are myriad other perspectives, myriad other subjective worlds, in addition to our own, and that our own is only one among the many. From them we see that the unclingable Spirit is a lover of rattlesnakes and armadillos as well as of faithful dogs and domesticated cats. Animals in the wild teach us that there is much that is nonhuman, untameable, and unmanipulable in God. They teach us to think of God as the very spirit of wilderness itself: like Kali in Hinduism, a cosmic lover who is herself ultimately good, but also beyond our superficial understandings of goodness.

**Animals as Images of God** The fifth way in which animals

can be seen in an ecological spirituality is as images of God. We are familiar with prehistoric, archaic, and primal religious traditions in which animals have been used as images of the divine life. The most famous image of divinity in Olmec civilization, for example, was that which merged a jaguar and a human, and in ancient Egypt the divine seems often to have been imaged as a cat. While appreciating biblical imagery of the divine as cosmic person, an ecological spirituality can recognize that there is truth in other imagery. Inasmuch as animals are part of the divine body, they do indeed reflect something of the content of the divine life, and inasmuch as we can experience God through them, we can sense something of the divine mystery by rendering the mystery in animal terms. If we do not absolutize the imagery, mistaking it for the living spirit, we can authentically speak of "God the Jaguar" and "God the divine Spider" as well as "God the Father" and "God the Mother." The latter imagery may be more meaningful for us, but the former imagery can help us to be skeptical of our own anthropocentrism, and to help us remember that God is the God of all life, not human life alone. Such creative imagery, too, will diverge from traditional Christianity, which has imaged God only by analogy to human persons. It may also help expand the horizons of Christian love, which is the very aim of an ecological spirituality.

As those of us who travel the path of an ecological spirituality internalize such ways of seeing animals, we will become increasingly cognizant of our bondedness with other animals. As this occurs, we will become increasingly troubled by our widespread oppression of individual animals under human dominion. We will realize that, after all, these animals are our own kin. For us, two questions will naturally emerge: How is an ethical concern for individual animals to be understood within the larger context of Christian social action? How important is it compared to concerns for other people and concerns for the earth? To these questions I now turn.

# Acting on Behalf of Domesticated Animals

An ecological spirituality takes as its ethical aim the promotion of societies that are socially just, ecologically sustainable, and spiritually satisfying. In the first chapter I included concern for the well-being of animals under the category of "ecological sustainability," since that category highlights our responsibilities to nature. At this point, however, we can add that a concern for animals can also be included under the heading "justice." The World Council of Churches report to which I alluded earlier puts it this way:

> Concern for animals is not a simple question of kindness, however laudable that virtue is. *It is an issue of strict justice.* In all our dealing with animals, whether direct or indirect, the ethic for the liberation of life requires that *we render unto animals what they are due, as creatures with an independent integrity and value.* Precisely because they cannot speak for themselves or act purposively to free themselves from the shackles of their enslavement, the Christian duty to speak and act for them is the greater, not the lesser.[4]

That we may not have considered "justice" applicable to animals has something to do with how we have conceived the "societies" in which we live. If we think un-ecologically, we think of societies as "human societies" and of "justice" as "justice for humans." It is as if we are insulated from nature, and nature from us, by an invisible boundary. If we think ecologically, however, no such boundary exists. We recognize that the societies in which we live include land, water, air and those animals which we have under our direct dominion; "justice" includes justice for all living beings within the society, not only human beings. The concern for animals is not only a concern for ecological sustainability; it is also a concern for social justice.

Still, many of us feel plagued by too many issues with which to be concerned. The addition of animals to our sphere of concern can seem like a depletion of our already limited energies. An ecological spirituality can look at the matter differently. If we are truly committed to an ethic of reverence for life, we will be on the lookout for ways in which justice for animals might also contribute to justice for people and for the earth, and acting in behalf of animals might empower us to have more energy for additional human and ecological concerns. To illustrate the first point, consider the following five reasons why a Christian might rightly become a vegetarian.

## Vegetarianism as an Act of Solidarity with the Earth and the Poor

For many of us, an ecological spirituality will rightly lead to the adoption of a vegetarian diet. I have been a meat-eater myself, and I know that the elimination of meat is not always easy. Indeed, it is quite difficult to become a vegetarian if you grow up in south Texas, as I did. In that part of the world numerous cultural influences will tell you that meat-eating is healthy, natural, and manly, and that vegetarianism is an odd diet for people who are overly sentimental about animals. Despite the power of Texas mythologies, however, I have come to believe that Christians and others in industrialized nations who seek societies that are just and sustainable ought to reduce our consumption of meat and dairy products as much as possible. Here are five reasons why those in the United States and Canada, at least, ought to do so. Combined, they illustrate how a concern for animals can complement a concern for other people and the earth.[5]

First, much of the grain which now goes to feed livestock could better be used to feed the poor. A billion people could be fed with the amount of grain and soybeans that now go to feed U.S. livestock. Ninety percent of the protein, ninety-nine percent of the carbohydrates, and one hundred percent of the fiber available for direct human consumption in grains and vegetables are wasted when cycled through livestock. If we had unlimited quantities of land, of course, such waste would not be a problem. But the earth does not have unlimited land. Given population projections, available land is used much more efficiently as cropland than as pasture for grazing. On the average, land used to supply grains and vegetables can feed twenty times more people than can an equivalent amount of land used as pasture to supply meat. Thus, if we want to contribute to a long-term solution to hunger, we ought to refrain from eating meat. This is an option, at least, for those of us in industrial nations, whose survival does not depend on the eating of meat.

Second, the North American meat habit is a driving force behind the destruction of the tropical forests. Annually, the United States alone imports almost two hundred million pounds of meat from Costa Rica, El Salvador, Guatemala, Nicaragua, Honduras, and Panama. Forests must be cleared to provide pasture land for the cattle. If we want to help save the these forests, it has been argued, we ought to do our part to stop our country's voracious import of beef.

Third, feedlots and slaughterhouses are major polluters of rivers and streams. U.S. livestock produce 250,000 pounds of excrement a second, and yet sewage systems in U.S. feedlots are practically nonexistent. It is estimated that ninety percent of the harmful organic waste water pollution in the United States is attributable to livestock. If we want to do our part to urge a cleaner environment, we ought to cease supporting the industries that pollute.

Fourth, a meat-based diet is itself a cause of many chronic diseases, not least of which are heart disease in men and breast cancer in women. It has been shown by nutritionists, as well as by the example of countless vegetarian civilizations throughout the world, that all the protein necessary for good health can be obtained through a vegetarian diet. If we want to do our own bodies and our loved ones a favor, we ought to to avoid a meat-based diet and considerably reduce our intake of dairy products.

Fifth, and finally, we ought to become vegetarian for the sake of the animals themselves. Of course, when we buy the corpses of these animals in supermarkets, we are enticed not to think of them as "animals." We think of them as "meat." They are packaged in ways that make us forget that once they had faces, hair, feet, and blood, much less capacities for pain and pleasure and goals of their own. Somewhere we have forgotten what our childhood hymn taught us: that "all things bright and beautiful, all creatures great and small" belong, not to us as our objects to use however we please, but rather to "the Lord God" who "made them all."

From the perspective of an ecological spirituality, the killing of animals per se is not the problem. At least we need not oppose the killing of animals if, as is the case on many small farms, the animals are allowed some kind of quality existence prior to slaughter, if the killing is done instantaneously, and if it is done in ways that cause minimum apprehension on the part of the animal. But few of the dead animals we can buy at the supermarket meet such criteria. Ol' MacDonald's family farm has quickly been replaced by the corporate meat-factory; the good shepherd by the agribusinessman. In the United States, almost all poultry products and half the milk and red meat come from large-scale indoor production, all of which is subsidized by government aid. The best way to end the inhumane treatment of such production is to cease consuming the products of the factory farms, buying meat only from sources where animals have been treated with respect.

Thus, the choice of vegetarianism is not a choice for the well-being of animals alone, important as that is. It is also a choice for the well-being of tropical forests, for healthy rivers and streams, for the long-term goal of feeding the world's hungry, and for bodily health. To say "no" to meat is to say "yes" to animals, other people, ourselves, and the earth. A preferential option for animals is simultaneously a preferential option for the earth and the poor.

## Vegetarianism as an Empowering Ritual

There is still another reason why vegetarianism can assist the ecological Christian in living a life of solidarity with the the earth and the poor. This pertains to the objection that concern for animals might deplete our already limited moral energies. At least in the case of vegetarianism, the opposite can be the case. The adoption of meatless diets can be a sacrament of sorts, a daily ritual in which we participate in divine yearnings for peace on earth, and in which, in so doing, we share in the very peace of God.

Considering our often-felt impotence to make a difference in the world, a daily ritual of vegetarianism can be uniquely empowering. Few have put this point as eloquently as the animal rights philosopher Tom Regan. Regan notes that when we choose the food on our plates, "we are faced with a direct personal choice, over which we exercise absolute sovereign authority."[6] Such choices are rare, because, though we wish the contrary, many of us have little if any influence "on the practices of the World Bank, the agrarian land-reform movement, the call to reduce armed conflicts, the cessation of famine and the evil of abject poverty." But with food on our plates it is different. "Here we are at liberty to exercise absolute control." With the simple act of lifting it to our mouths, our fork can be a sword or a plowshare. What shall we do?

> When we consider the biographical and, I dare say, the spiritual kinship we share with those billions of animals raised and slaughtered for food; when, further, we inform ourselves of the truly wretched conditions in which most of these animals are raised, not to mention the deplorable methods by which they are transported and the gruesome, blood-soaked reality of the slaughterhouse; and when, finally, we take honest stock of our privileged position in the world, a position that will not afford us the excuse from moral blame shared by the desperately poor...when we

consider all these factors, then the case for abstaining from animal flesh has the overwhelming weight of both impartial reason and a spiritually-infused compassion.[7]

Christians opting for vegetarianism can themselves become spirituality- infused, to use Regan's metaphor, and then use the energy of this infusion to help others, people included, to enjoy the fruits of justice, peace, and respect for the integrity of creation. In this way a respect for animals, exercised through compassionate use of the fork, can be understood as a daily starting point for empowering us to be concerned with other issues, with justice for humans and with sustainability for the earth.

## Additional Responses to the Abuse of Animals

Although I have just suggested that the adoption of vegeterianism can serve the poor and the earth as well as animals, and that it can be an empowering ritual, it is important to affirm that sometimes we must act simply for the sake of animals, even though there is no additional benefit for us. The following lifestyle changes, suggested at the World Council of Churches consultation, are desirable even though they have no clear benefits to any besides the animals.

1. Avoid cosmetics and household products that have been cruelly tested on animals.
2. Avoid clothing and other aspects of fashion that have a history of cruelty to animals, products of the fur industry in particular.
3. Avoid patronizing forms of entertainment that treat animals as mere means to human ends. Instead, seek benign forms of entertainment, ones that nurture a sense of the wonder of God's creation and reawaken that duty of conviviality we can discharge by living respectfully in community with all life, the animals included.[8]

This is not to say that all uses of animals are to be avoided. Sometimes animals may indeed need to be used, albeit with respect. This, I believe, is the case with certain forms of medical research. In such research, however, attempts must be made by researchers themselves to reduce the numbers of animals used as much as possible, to replace animals with alternatives (e.g., computer models, tissue cultures) wherever possible, and to refine techniques so that animals are subjected to minimum discomfort and given ample opportunity to enjoy a satisfactory existence. The greater the capacities for sentience in the animals at issue, the more reluctant we must be to sanction their use. Even in medical research, there is no justification whatsoever for pain or torment.

Needless to say, the adoption of lifestyle changes such as those just mentioned is best complemented by efforts to change the systems and institutions that allow or perpetuate animal abuse. Christians concerned with factory farms, for example, can urge an end to tax-supported research and technological developments of intensive research methods; they can demand the development of local markets where farmers committed to humane treatment of animals can trade directly with consumers; and they can insist upon meatless meals and non-factory farm products from restaurants, hotels, airliners, school lunch services, and churches. Institutions, too, must be changed.

A starting point for institutional change is the church. Christians are not individuals in isolation, but individuals in community. Ideally, churches are the places where our deepest capacities for compassion are nourished, and where we discover what it truly means to live the Christian life. Even if we do not experience our churches this way, we have an obligation to change them, and thus to live up to the bold claim that we are "people of God." Practically speaking, this means that we should urge our churches to seek social justice and ecological sustainability, and to recognize that a respect for individual animals is one part of this larger commitment. In addition, we should pressure our respective denominations to place animal welfare concerns on their agendas for national meetings. Given that most churches are currently far from this recognition, much consciousness raising is needed. Within churches, the animal welfare movement is probably where the women's movement was twenty years ago. Both have a terribly long way to go. But consciousness raising must begin somewhere. If we recognize that we, as individual Christians, are sinners, that we fall far short of the glory of God even if we do respect animals, and that those who do not respect animals may nevertheless better approximate God's glory than do we, then that consciousness raising begins with us, the readers of this book. Of course, consciousness raising is more than mere words. It is action. Indeed, perhaps our consciousness raising begins with the very next meal we eat.

## Questions for Reflection and Discussion

1. If you have been shaped by a Christian tradition, how have animals been conceived in this tradition? Are there any ideas in this tradition, perhaps neglected in this chapter, which might enhance our capacities to respect animals? What ideas proposed in this chapter, if any, directly conflict with the teachings of your tradition?

2. Review the five ways of perceiving animals proposed in this chapter. Which are most controversial? Which are most conducive to a respect for animals? Which, if any, are most difficult for you to accept? Why?

3. In your view, are human beings justified in domesticating animals for *any* purposes? On what basis are they justified?

4. Does an emphasis on divine love for animals undermine or enrich a recognition of divine love for humans? Explain your answer.

5. Review the difference between intrinsic and instrumental

value. Do you agree that there are degrees of intrinsic value among organisms?

6. Consider the arguments for vegetarianism in this chapter. Do you agree that Christians who seek to be "open to animals" ought to adopt a vegetarian diet? Why or why not?

# Openness
# to the Earth

> This we know: the
> earth does not belong to man, man belongs to the earth.
> Man did not weave the web of life; he is merely a strand in
> it. Whatever he does to the web, he does to himself....If
> men spit on the ground, they spit on themselves.
>
> Chief Seattle

Chief Seattle's warning is auspicious. Today humanity is indeed spitting on the ground, and with substances much more dangerous than saliva. Consider Love Canal, New York. Around 1978 the people of this community discovered an unusual number of cancers and birth defects in their midst. After investigations, they discovered that the diseases were the result of irresponsible practices of the Hooker Chemical Company, which from the late 1940s had used the site to dump dioxin, lindane, and mirex. The company had spit on the ground. It took only thirty years for the chemical to seep through the soil and contaminate the water supply of the community. Thousands of people still suffer the health consequences of this irresponsible dumping of toxic wastes.[1]

But Love Canal is by no means an isolated incident. In the United States alone, industries release almost 250 million tons of toxic waste each year. This amounts to almost one ton a person. Increasingly, the United States and other First World countries are seeking Third World countries as the dumping grounds for these wastes. In addition, the United States produces almost eight billion dollars a year of pesticides, many of which are suspected of causing cancer and birth defects, two-fifths of which are exported, often to developing countries. Of these exports, one-quarter is made of chemicals whose use is severely restricted or banned at home. Thus the United States contributes to an ever widening "circle of poison."

The problem runs deep. It is not simply that we fail to take sufficient precautions, that we have lacked technological expertise. Rather, it is that we are shaped by an unecological and destructive way of approaching the earth, of which our absence of precautions are but a symptom. Through the unecological paradigm that has been part of the modern Western world, we approach the earth as a mere dumping ground for our waste and a mere instrument for our purposes. We treat it as a spitoon.

An ecological spirituality will bear witness to a quite different way of feeling the presence of the earth. Inasmuch as we internalize this spirituality, we feel moved to join David Brower, founder of Friends of the Earth, in a new pledge of allegiance, a planetary pledge:

> I owe an allegiance to the planet that has made me possible, and to all the life on that planet, whether friendly or not. I also owe an allegiance to the three and one half billion years of life that made it possible for me to be here, and all the rest of you.[2]

With many environmentalists, we will see that we have a responsibility not only to ourselves, but also to future human generations, "to the hundreds of billions of people who have not yet been born, who have a right to be, who deserve a world at least as beautiful as ours, whose genes are now in our custody and no one else's."[3] And we will have a responsibility to nonhuman generations as well, to the myriad species who, like ourselves, add to the divine life. We will feel the earth as the body of God rather than an object of indifference, as the recipient of gratitude rather than a repository of spit.

When we speak of "the earth," of course, we can mean different things. We can mean the globe on which we live; we can mean the inorganic materials—solid, gaseous, and liquid—of which this globe is composed; and we can mean one particular aspect of these materials; namely, the solid ground on which we stand. In short, we can mean the planet, its matter, or the land. An ecological spirituality will be sensitive to the earth in each of its three aspects. It will view the planet as our home; it will see matter as alive with intrinsic value; and it will see land as a subject of kindly use.

As Thomas Berry points out in the Foreword, the social and ecological importance of a spirituality of the earth cannot be overemphasized. Waste disposal is by no means the only problem we face. Our global population threatens to exceed the earth's carrying capacity; our consumption of renewable and nonrenewable resources threatens to extinguish its limited supplies and further to destroy the habitats of countless species; our industrial practices threaten to alter its climate. The problems are not in the First World alone, or in the First World's disposal of wastes on the Third World. As Kenyan journalist Calestous Juma comments:

> Africa is full of lonely peasants; millions of people alienated from one another by the destruction of nature....Forests recede day after day and the peasants walk farther and farther for firewood. As the rivers and springs dry up more

often, they walk farther and farther for water. As the land gets degraded, the lonely peasant toils only to harvest less year after year....Those threads that tie the peasants to nature are...deep-rooted: their disruption leaves severe wounds on the health and collective consciousness of the people. The lonely peasant is a grim reminder to the rest of humanity of the ultimate implications of a lonely planet.[4]

It is almost as if people all over the world are waging a battle against the earth: out of choice in the case of the powerful, and out of necessity in the case of the powerless. All over the world we are neglecting the fact that, as Chief Seattle put it, the earth does not belong to us; rather, we belong to the earth. It is for the sake of a true peace on earth, which is a peace *with* the earth, that we must develop a spirituality of the earth. The first feature of such a spirituality is that it is sensitive to the "aliveness of matter."

## The Aliveness of Matter

Many of us think of matter as defined by the dictionary: "the substance of which a physical object is composed." Let us accept this definition. For a spirituality of the earth, the problem comes with an assumption concerning the nature of this matter.

Consciously or unconsciously, we often divide the world of matter into two types, living matter and dead matter, assuming that plants and animals are composed of the former, and that rocks and submicroscopic elements are composed of the latter. If we have been especially influenced by mechanistic thought, we may also believe that living matter can ultimately be reduced to dead matter, and hence that the physical world, including its plants and animals, is a vast system of lifeless particles-in-motion.

What do "living" and "dead" mean in this context? An entity is "living," so we assume, if it prehends, or takes into account, a surrounding environment from its own subjective perspective, either consciously or subconsciously, and perhaps also if it partially determines its own destiny, and thus creates itself in responding to that environment. Almost always we assume that human beings, while alive, are living in these two senses. We believe that they are sentient, which is to say that they feel the presence of their environments, and we believe that they are at least to some extent free, which is to say that they creatively respond to what they feel. If we are asked, we might also concede that other animals are sentient and creative, and, if pressed, we might even claim this of living cells. But here we would draw the line. The inorganic arena, so we would claim, is neither sentient nor creative. Rocks and other inorganic realities, so we often believe, are "dead."

The spirituality of matter proposed in this work proceeds from a different perspective. It follows the perspective of Alfred North Whitehead and others, ancient as well as modern, who assume that "dead" matter is, in its own, unconscious way, "living." Representatives of this perspective include, in different ways and contexts, African traditionalists, Native Americans, ancient Greeks, numerous Asian thinkers, Romantic poets from the West, and modern Western thinkers such as Leibniz, Goethe, and the nineteenth-century essayist, John Ruskin.

Consider, for example, the views of Ruskin as articulated in *The Ethics of Dust*.[5] In this work, ostensibly a dialogue with a young friend on crystals, Ruskin reveals some of his own deepest convictions concerning physical matter. His young interlocutor asks him if mountains can be conceived as living, and Ruskin replies:

> You may at least earnestly believe that the presence of the spirit, which culminates in your own life, shows itself in dawning, wherever the dust of the earth begins to assume any orderly and lovely state....Things are not either wholly alive, or wholly dead. They are less or more alive.[6]

The mountain, so Ruskin suggests, *is* alive, though less alive than the young man asking the question. There are, he submits, degrees of aliveness.

Whitehead would agree with Ruskin. Much of Whitehead's later philosophy was devoted to a repudiation of the idea that there are "vacuous actualities," that is, actualities which are only objects for observers, without any sense of being subjects for themselves. Whitehead believed it plausible, and indeed more reasonable than not, to assume that reality at any and every level consists of actualities that possess some degree of subjectivity. "Apart from the experience of subjects," he said, "there is nothing, nothing, nothing, bare nothingness."[7]

Why did he believe this? There are at least two reasons. First, taking evolution seriously, Whitehead found it implausible to assume that, for billions of years in cosmic evolution, there were only "dead" objects, be they protons, neutrons, and other such objects, and that then, somewhat miraculously on the planet earth, the "living" emerged from these dead objects. Just as the Greeks thought that "something" cannot come from "nothing," so Whitehead believed that the "living" cannot come from the "dead"; the living can only come from the alive. Hence, for Whitehead, it seemed more plausible than not to assume that the precursors to biological life on earth—subatomic particles and their aggregates—were themselves alive in some sense. Given Whitehead's line of thinking, inorganic realities are best understood as primitive expressions of, rather than exceptions to, what later in the evolutionary process we call "life."

Second, taking contemporary physics seriously, Whitehead found it reasonable to assume that, at bottom, the submicroscopic arena consists, not of "particles" and "waves," but rather of momentary pulsations of energy: energy-events. Particles and waves are themselves composed of such momentary events. As quantum mechanics shows, these events possess the very two properties characteristic of life as defined above. In coming into being, they "take into account" past events, thus exemplifying a capacity to prehend the past; and they "respond" to the very events they take into account, thus exemplifying a capacity for creativity. They are in their own way creative and sentient, the earliest instances in our cosmic epoch of what we call subjective experience.

For Whitehead, then, as for Ruskin, a mountain is alive. As Whitehead would see it, a mountain is a massive expression of billions of energy-events, each of which, on occurrence, has its own subjective immediacy. Undoubtedly, the subjectivity of a subatomic energy-event is radically different from a momentary experience of animal life, including human life. A subatomic energy-event takes into account and thus prehends its predecessors, but in all probability it does not do so consciously or with the kind of sentience characteristic of animals with central nervous systems. And as it takes into account these predecessors, the energy-event creatively actualizes certain possibilities for response, though it probably does not do so with the kind of anticipation or mentation that is characteristic of human life. When climbing a mountain or stepping on a rock, which is itself composed of countless energy-events, we need not worry about causing the mountain pain, or offending the rock's sensibilities. But we can perceive the mountain and rock as something more than inert stuff. We can perceive it as an expression of living energy or vibrant matter, as a primitive form of aliveness.

What would this way of perceiving be like? At root, the mode of perception at issue is aesthetic. William Barrett, a philosopher best known for introducing existentialist philosophy to the West, can be our guide.

In his *Time of Need: Forms of the Imagination in the Twentieth Century*, Barrett surveys the history of the theme of nihilism as it is expressed and dealt with in twentieth-century Western literature. His subjects include Hemingway, Faulkner, Kafka, Camus, Ionesco, Joyce, and E. M. Forster. Working through Barrett's treatment of these authors, we are struck, as is he, by the fact that so many of the authors see the alienation of Western humanity from the natural world as a root cause and symptom of the nihilist dilemma.

In a subsequent work, *The Illusion of Technique,* Barrett again returns to the theme of nihilism as it is dealt with, and responded to, by twentieth- century Western philosophers. Here his subjects are Wittgenstein, Heidegger, and William James. What is interesting about Barrett's treatment is not simply that, again, he finds alienation from nature as a root symptom and cause of the phenomenon of Western nihilism, but that he discusses the problem of nihilism within himself. "What do I believe?," he asks after having dealt with the other philosophers. "As a philosopher, I would seem especially equipped to give an answer here, and yet my profession may be just the thing that screens me off from the human intent that lies behind the question. A philosopher may be able to reel off his ideas by the yard and yet remain blind to the things that really keep him going in life. What, then, do I live by?—that is the question, and in its grip every one of us stands on the same ground."[8]

Finding his own meaning in and through religious experience, Barrett explains that, for him and for many others, it has been no easy matter to dwell in a religious ambience in an age dominated by technical reason. "We cannot will back a faith that has been lost. We shall have to live back into that way of being in whose ambience the religious once drew breath. We shall have to find ourselves within nature before God is able to find us."[9]

The last sentence captures the heart of Barrett's own journey. He has had to find himself in nature before God is able to find him. Part of his own discovery has involved walks in the woods during the heart of winter, and it is on these walks that a sense for the aliveness of matter—even so-called dead matter—has been cultivated. From Barrett's own intuitions we have much to learn in seeking a spirituality of the earth.

Note first how he describes the disclosures during these walks of trees, creatures which we ordinarily take to be living:

Rocks and trees. I have grown to know them particularly

this winter; they have accompanied me on my walks, or rather I have learned to enter into their company. Winter trees are more beautiful than under the fat and heavy foliage of summer. Now they lay bare their secret structure, the naked and living line of branch and bough, the supple harshness of their enduring struggle with the elements. Oak, maple ash, chestnut, beech—these are now without their telltale leaves, and I have had to learn to read them by their barks, each as individual as fingerprints. With some I have come to know the particular curves and twists of their branches like the individual features of friends.[10]

Next we do well to attend to the way he describes his other companions on the winter walk, the rocks:

Whoever thinks matter is mere inert stuff has not looked long at rocks. They do not lie inert; they thrust forward, or crouch back in quiet self-gathered power. Like a cat sitting so still that his tail has ceased twitching. Only Cezanne, among artists, did rocks properly, painting them into the canvas as alive as the trees against which he sets them. In the gray light of winter they come alive in their color too—smoke-gray or blue-gray, molded and subtle in their shading that shifts as the gray light shifts. The living rock! More than an idle phrase. Out of the living rock the waters of spirit.[11]

What is significant about Barrett's description is that he, like Cezanne, perceives the rocks, not as utterly lifeless compared to the trees, but rather as ontologically continuous with the trees. Barrett sees rocks "as alive as the trees."

An ecological Christian can add that rocks are alive in different ways from trees. In all probability, the mode of subjectivity present in an electron-event within the depths of an atom is qualitatively different from that present in a living cell in a tree, and both are different from that present within the psyches of advanced organisms such as porpoises and chimpanzees. To say that all creatures are alive is not to say that they are all alive in the same ways.

Moreover, to say that they are alive is not to say that they are alive to the same degree. With Ruskin we can say that rocks—or, more particularly, the pulsations of vibrant energy of which they are composed—are less sentient in terms of their capacities for rich experience than are tree cells, whose capacities for richness are probably less than those of animal psyches. An entity's capacity for rich experience can be measured in terms of its capacity to experience various items within its environment with harmonious intensity. Complex forms of bodily organization, such as sense receptors and nervous systems, enhance an entity's capacity to experience variety with intensity, and thus enhance its capacity for experiential richness. But no entities, not even rocks, are totally devoid of subjectivity and its attendant richness. No entities, not even rocks, are utterly lifeless and therefore devoid of intrinsic value. If Christians are to discover a spirituality of the earth, they do well to internalize William Barrett's intuitions, which mirror the intuitions of so many cultures. They will discover that in certain ways rocks, and indeed all physical matter, are alive.

From the point of view of an ecological Christianity, to see physical matter as alive is to see it as God sees it. God sees and appreciates things as they are; if inorganic realities are in certain ways alive, then God will perceive and appreciate them accordingly. God will feel their inward natures empathetically, that is, with a subjective attunement that mirrors and shares in the very inwardness by which the inorganic realities are imbued. God will recognize, as might we, that the earth itself is sacred.

To say that the earth is sacred, at least as I use the word sacred in this work, is not to say that the earth is identical with God, although certainly, as will be discussed subsequently, it is a part of God's identity. Nor is it to say that God is in the earth, although indeed, as will also be discussed subsequently, such is the case. Rather, it is to say that in different ways relative to its different constituents, the earth is of intrinsic value, and this value deserves our care and reverence. A spirituality of the earth begins with an inwardly felt sense that the very matter of which we are composed, and upon which we are dependent, is sacred. It begins with a realization that energy is living, that in certain mysterious ways it has value for itself, and that, as Barrett observes, it is out of this energy, out of this living rock, that the waters of spirit emerge.

## Kindly Use of the Land

Important as it is to recognize the earth's intrinsic value, however, a spirituality of the earth cannot stop here. Inevitably, the earth is something we use, and hence something that has instrumental value for us. A spirituality of the earth can and should recognize this instrumentality, and seek to discern its connection to God.

For the sake of discovering this connection, it is helpful to focus on one feature of the earth which for at least seven thousand years our species has been using with increasing vigor, sometimes benignly and sometimes not. Let us focus on the land, understood as the ground on which we stand, and, more particularly, as the soil which, since the dawn of agriculture, we have been farming. Indeed it is this ground from whose dust, so the Bible tells us, we were made, and over which, so it also says, we have a certain dominion (Genesis 1:28).

What is the soil? From the scientist's perspective, it is the surface area of the earth, from a few inches to several feet thick, consisting of small particles of rocks and minerals broken down by water, wind, and land movements, and of microscopic and macroscopic organisms such as fungi, beetles, and earthworms. From the farmer's point of view, it is something to be tilled, plowed, and cultivated, so that it might yield plant life by which we ourselves can be nurtured. And from anyone's perspective, it can rightly be understood as something to be seen, touched, and smelled, revealing its own textures and colors, and suggesting something sacred. Of course, this something cannot be understood atomistically. Soil does not exist as a self-enclosed substance isolated from other realities; its own texture and structure exist in relation to, and are influenced by, vegetation, the rock material from which it has emerged, and the climate in which it is situated. But amid this relationality the soil, like any other matter, has intrinsic value. In different ways and degrees, its organic and inorganic components are expressive of living energy.

Yet the soil also has instrumental value, and not simply to humans. Consider plants. The soil has instrumental value to them as a foundation on which to grow and as a reservoir of water and other nutrients. Historically, the first plants to have colonized it were blue-green algae and lichens. Millions of years ago they converted nitrogen from the atmosphere into nitrates; they transformed carbon dioxide and water into complex starches. In so doing they created, and continue to create, a setting within which they themselves can flourish, and within which other kinds of plants and animals can live. Upon decomposition, these plants and animals create that "humus" upon which still more developed forms of plants depend, plants which are in turn consumed by more developed animals. Quite independent of any reference to humans, a study of nature shows that plants and animals are of instrumental value to one another, and that both depend upon, and hence use, that vital asset which we name "the soil." In their own way, they, too, have "dominion" over the earth.

Bringing humans into the picture, we see that our agriculture can best be understood as one way in which we, too, use the soil. Of course we do not eat the soil; rather we eat plants and animals that depend on the soil. In agriculture we use the soil in order to cultivate those plants and animals upon whom we depend for our survival. Plowing, sowing, tilling, and harvesting are all instances of such use.

Of late, our degree and methods of use have far exceeded the well-being of the soil itself. Our use has become abuse, effected through unsustainable forms of agriculture that cause erosion, and through excessive urban development which covers available cropland. According to the United Nations report published in the mid-1970s, "the present rate of soil loss through erosion may be as high as 2500 metric tons per year—over half a ton of soil for every man, woman, and child on the planet."[12] Since the dawn of agricultural civilizations 7000 years ago, one-half of the earth's food-producing soil has disappeared, and it is estimated that by the year 2000 one-third of the remaining soil will be lost.[13]

These alarming rates of soil erosion do not bode well for the world's poor. As Lester Brown puts it, "If this soil depletion is not soon checked, persistent pockets of famine are likely to appear."[14] Indeed, in many parts of the world, these pockets have already appeared. Those who have died need not have died if appropriate agricultural policies had been in place, along with, of course, just economic and political systems.

## Sustainable Agriculture

The long term solution to the problem of soil erosion is the adoption on the part of farmers of a sustainable agriculture. As David Katz points out, when a farmer does this, he or she adopts an approach to the land that "emphasizes stewardship and understanding of the internal relationships of the agroecosystem, stressing long-term conservation of resources rather than maximizing production of a single crop." The farmer "selects strategies that attempt to balance the need for high yields each year with the longer term biological requirements that will lead to ecological sustainability."[15] These strategies are, of course, strategies for *use*. They are premised on the idea that the land is, and should be, a resource for human utilization. But they are, in Wendell Berry's phrase, strategies for "kindly use."

As Katz points out, they involve nutrient management, a careful husbanding of the soil, and the building of stability.

Nutrient management "concentrates on building up the biological fertility of the soil, so that crops take the nutrients they need from the steady turnover within the soil reservoir." Fertilizers can be used for nutrient management, but those that are highly soluble should be used "carefully and sparingly."[16] In general, it is preferable that the waste products from the crops themselves form the nutrients from which subsequent crops can draw. The nutrients are best managed by allowing the natural forces to manage themselves.

Careful husbanding of the soil involves an attempt to avoid deterioration of the soil. Tillage systems are chosen to minimize impacts such as erosion, compaction, and oxidation; the soil is kept under cover as much as possible, with extensive use being made of legume rotations, cover crops, and green manures. The "overall goal is to use the soil as a fertility bank for future generations where the deposits always surpass the withdrawals."[17]

The building of stability involves a concern for the complexity and diversity of life forms that are necessary for a stable, and hence sustainable, agroecological system. Such building implies "the maintenance of a wide range of plant types and habitats on the farm," and it also implies "the utilization of a sophisticated understanding of population dynamics in order to manipulate host/pest/predator relationships among the organisms in the ecosystem without causing major disruptions." The practices that enhance stability include growing host plants as food for beneficial insects, using trap crops and strip planting, and planting shelter belts and hedgerows. Amid such practices, pesticides may sometimes be used, but with caution and sparcity. The aim is to "avoid as much contamination or disrupton of the ecosystem as possible."

Of course, we cannot ask farmers to adopt such practices unless it is economically feasible for them to do so, and unless those of use who can afford to do so share in whatever sacrifices are necessary. Katz observes, "if long-term sustainability is to become a major criterion for our farmers, major changes in our society's economic and political systems must occur."[18] For these changes to occur, major shifts in our cultural values are required. Industrial societies are noted for their celebration of urban/industrial values and their neglect of rural values. Urban/industrial values are expressed in the six characteristics of industrial society identified by the cultural historian Alvin Toffler: standardization, specialization, synchronization, concentration, maximization, and centralization. They result in that "technicist" mentality which has its spiritual underpinnings in an inwardly-felt but often unacknowledged impulse to dominate and subjugate the world: a will-to-power. As Wendell Berry points out, unsustainable agriculture has itself been industrialized, thus diminishing the rural values that once were characteristic of the farming communities. At best, these values involve a respect for physical labor, self-reliance, physical health, honesty, and practical ingenuity. A sustainable agriculture requires a society that deems these values worthy.

The needed changes in social and political structure on the one hand, and social values on the other, must have a spiritual underpinning other than the will-to-power. And yet the spirituality at issue must not be a romantic spirituality of *no use*. It must be one of *kindly use*, or, to use a word used by Jews and Christians of an ecological orientation, "stewardship." A spirituality of the earth involves, not only a respect for the earth's intrinsic value, but a "stewardly" approach to its usefulness.

It is very important to distinguish stewardship from a mere prudent management of nature. A healthy and biblically nourished idea of stewardship will not see nature as an alien substance from which we are detached and which we can manipulate at will. Rather—along with the first chapters of Genesis (2:4-4:16), various psalms (8, 19, 74, 104), passages from Isaiah (40:12-31, 45:9-13, 48:12-13) and Jeremiah (27:5 and 32:17), and themes from wisdom literature (Proverbs 3:19-20, 8:22-31)—it will recognize that humans are a part of, rather than apart from, nature. Indeed, it will recognize that the very word "nature," if used to refer to a realm from which human beings are excluded, is foreign to biblical points of view, and that the common idea that humans are of an ontological order that is discontinuous from the rest of creation is neither ecological nor biblical. An ecologically sensitive expression of stewardship will begin with the assumption shared by biblical perspectives and process theology; namely, that humans are united with their fellow creatures in being part of a single ontological order: an order named "the creation."

## Two Meanings of Creation

In this work I have used the word "nature" not to refer to a realm apart from the human, but rather to refer to a realm of which humans are a part. It is used synonymously with the word "creation." To speak of nature, ourselves included, as a creation says at least two things. First, it is to say that we are united with our fellow creatures—including the land and its soil—in mutual dependence upon God. Second, it is to say that we are united as mutual subjects of God's love. In order to clarify the nature of a stewardship as it can be appropriately exercised, a brief word about each of these meanings is in order.

Dependence upon God can be understood as a dependence upon that divine lure which has called creation into existence in the past through the process of evolution, and which calls us, and our fellow creatures as well, into the fullness of life in the present. God has created and continues to create the world through persuasion rather than coercion, evocation rather than manipulation, invitation rather than compulsion. Stated another way, God has created and continues to create the world, not by molding passive "matter" into preconceived and rigid forms, but rather by calling active and free existents into forms of order and growth that are possible for them in the situations at hand. The creatures of the world, human and nonhuman, are united as co-responders to this call: responders who sometimes hit and sometimes miss the mark of appropriate response. Together, we humans and our fellow creatures "depend" on God, not as passive clay depends on a potter for externally imposed form, but rather as living beings depend on the sun for life-nourishing possibilities. As responders to God's call, we are all on the same ontological level: that of dependent, and yet free and creative, creatures.

It is important to note that this dependence is neither exclusive nor unilateral. It is not exclusive because we depend for our existence not only on God's lure, but also also on the myriad other beings who have responded to that lure in the past, and indeed upon myriad other beings in the present as well. We have not simply been created by God, we have been co-created by God and by distant kin. A relational ontology such as that proposed in this work cannot rest content with simple dependence; it recognizes by contrast that we are dependent upon many things, and indeed upon everything.

Furthermore, our dependence is not unilateral because, even as we depend upon God, God also depends upon us. At any given stage in natural history, including human history, the efficacy of God's call depends in part on the faithfulness of creaturely response. We cannot simply look at everything that has been produced in evolution, or everything that happens in human life, and behold it as an effect of divine creative power. We must also recognize that things have happened and continue to happen that even God cannot control. Even as the world depends upon God, so God depends on the world. What makes God "God" is not that the world exists in a state of absolute dependence upon divine power, as if God were nothing more than a cosmic despot, a divine Caesar. Rather, what makes God "God" is that all creatures exist as subjects of God's all-tender and all-faithful love. God may be the most powerful reality there is, and that reality by whom all creatures will finally be redeemed, but God is not an all-powerful reality. For Christians,

God is best understood, not as a cosmic despot who can manipulate things at will, but rather as the One revealed in Jesus'
death on the cross, the one whose power includes vulnerability
and unlimited love.

This is the second implication of speaking of nature as creation. To say that we are united with the rest of the earth, including the land and its soil, as instances of creation is to say that
we, together with the rest of nature, are loved by God. To be a
creature is to be something that God recognized long ago, and
still recognizes, as *good*. This "goodness" is the intrinsic value of
the creature. It is the creature as it exists in itself and for itself, as
beheld and loved by God. In the case of land, this "goodness"
would be the subjectivity of organic creatures in the soil, and it
would be that primal aliveness which is constitutive of the energy-events within the depths even of inorganic matter. According to H. Wheeler Robinson, it is toward such aliveness that biblical perspectives also point in their understandings of the earth.
From their point of view, "Earth itself is alive....The earth has its
nature, which makes itself felt and demands respect."[19] Indeed,
"nature is alive through and through, and therefore the more capable of sympathy with [humanity], and of response to the rule
of its Creator and Upholder, on whom it directly depends."[20]

A "stewardly" approach to the earth, and in this case to the
soil, will proceed on the basis of these assumptions concerning
creation. As the soil is used, it will be seen as dependent upon
God in the sense of being, in its own ways, a co-responder to
God's call, and as a subject of God's love. For both these reasons, the steward will feel a sense of unity with it. If we are the
stewards, we will realize that we have been made from—or perhaps better, called from—the dust of the ground, or some analogous material substratum, and that in an evolutionary context
this substratum, perhaps the soil itself, has itself been called into
existence. Our use of the soil involves one facet of creation using
another. Moreover, we will see that we are very much dependent on the soil that we use, as we are on almost every other fac-

et of creation. Our existence on earth is indebted to soil and inseparable from it. Out of our sense that we are united with the soil, and that we are dependent upon it even as we are dependent upon God, we will try to make use of it kindly.

Stewardship, then, is not wanton exploitation or even efficient management. Rather it is kindly use. Amid such use we recognize that the soil is of intrinsic value, but we also see that it is an instrument for human purposes, specifically for agriculture. It is a "gift" to us even as it has life for itself. It is a gift in the sense that it is given to our species, and other species as well, from out of the evolutionary past, and in the sense that it is a godsend, an unasked for and unmerited foundation for our existence and that of other creatures. Inasmuch as God is responsible for the gift through the long and gradual processes of inorganic evolution, God is the giver of the gift. The gift of the soil is an expression of God's grace.

Our realization that the soil is a gift to us and to our fellow creatures should be complemented by a realization that we humans can be gifts to the soil. Just as the soil can be an instrument for our purposes, so we can be an instrument for its well-being. Through sustainable agriculture we serve as this instrument by acting to preserve and maintain its health and integrity. Unlike the soil, we exercise our instrumentality with conscious purpose, aware of other options. We consciously choose to be the caretaker and shepherd of the soil, and it is in this choice, fully aware of other options, that we mirror God's own way of being, God's own graceful consciousness. It is in this sense—as beings capable of consciously choosing to preserve and protect the earth—that we are made in God's image. Evolutionarily we have evolved into creatures who, perhaps alone or perhaps with other creatures, share with God a unique capacity: the capacity to feel the whole of creation as a beloved "we" in which there are no "theys," and then to act consciously on the basis of that feeling. We are made in God's image, not because we can exploit, but rather that we can care as God cares. Or at least we can try to do so, in our own ways and given our own capacities, and then act on the basis of such care.

## The Earth as God's Body

One of the most immediate products of the earth for which we can have stewardly care is our own bodies. Our bodies are the "temple of God," as Paul puts it. A recognition that our bodies are God's temple can remind us of two things.

First, it can remind us that a proper care for our bodies through nutrition and exercise is one way, and indeed a very important way, in which we can glorify God. It is no accident that medieval Christians identified sloth and gluttony as among the seven deadly sins. When those of us in affluent nations fail to care for our bodies, we are indeed "missing the mark" of responding to God's call toward wholeness. Our sins include eating and drinking the wrong kinds of foods, and ingesting even the right kinds of foods in quantities that far exceed our needs. And of course our sins also include the use of substances such as cigarettes and drugs that poison the very temple in which God dwells. The results of such sin, in terms of heart disease and cancer, are indeed deadly. Conversely, the results of conversion, in which we turn around from these habits and allow our bodies to develop in a healthy manner, yield a kind of fullness of life toward which we are beckoned by God.

Second, a recognition that our bodies are God's temple can remind us that a "kindly use" of our bodies through meditative exercises such as Hindu yoga or Zen zazen, or through dance and physical exercise, is one way that we can discover God. If God is in our bodies, sharing bodily experience with us, then we can open ourselves to God through proper use and enjoyment of our bodies.

As is implied by the phrase "use and enjoy our bodies," we are not simply identical with our bodies, nor are we simply different. Rather we are both identical and different. We are identical with our bodies in the sense that our bodies are a primary means through which we express ourselves and act in the world, and in the sense that bodily happenings partially determine our own destinies. What happens in and to our bodies, after all, happens in and to us. Yet we are different from our bodies in the sense that, as conscious subjects, we can be aware of our bodies as complex organisms—composed of cells, tissues, and organs—with lives of their own.

A person's difference from his or her body is evident in disease. The fact that my body has a life of its own is expressed in the fact that it can, after all, contract diseases which I, as a psyche, do not will or choose. My body can do things which I, as psyche, would have otherwise. Yet the very fact that the disease is my disease as well, affecting my consciousness and destiny, shows that, at least in this life, my own existence is enfleshed. Moreover, my own mental attitudes can partially influence and shape my body's healing and well-being. The truth is that my body is part of me, and yet more than me, and that I, in being able to influence my body, am part of my body, and yet more than it. My body and I are parts of one another, each immanent within one another and each transcending one another. In the language of Hua-Yen Buddhism, we are "mutually penetrating."

Of course, the relation of "mutual penetration" is not limited to that of psyche and body. With its emphasis on internal relations, an ecological Christianity can affirm that all things are mutually penetrating. The essence of any given thing is implicated in the essence of everything else, and vice-versa. The universe is a seamless web of existence in which all things are enfolded into the constitutions of all other things.

It is important that a spirituality of the earth recognize that such relationality and mutual enfoldment pertain even to God. Each creature in the universe is "in" God as the immediate subject of God's own experience, much in the way that a given portion of one's body can be "in" one's consciousness as the immediate subject of its experience. And just as we normally feel portions of our own bodies with empathy, so God feels each portion of the universe with empathy. God is the supremely sentient being: the ultimate instance of that life by which, as suggested above, even brute matter is characterized. God feels each creature's inward reality in its immanent relation with every other creature, and, in so doing, shares in each and every creature's destiny. Put simply, God is the psyche, the heart, of the universe, and the universe is God's body.

A recognition that the universe is God's body can complete that spirituality of the earth which has been discussed in this chapter. So far we have said that a spirituality of the earth is rooted in two intuitions: a recognition of the sacredness or intrinsic value of physical matter, and a recognition that the land is an evolutionary and divinely donated "gift" to be used according to biblical understandings of stewardship. To these two intuitions we can add a recognition that the earth, including what is external to our own bodies and what is internal to them, is God's own body. Rocks, wind, water, and fire are part of God's body, and so are the atoms, molecules, cells, and organs which constitute our own bodies. Our own bodies, and we ourselves, are part of that larger body which is the immediate content of God's own experience, and hence the content of God's own life.

As we learn to see the earth as God's body, we cultivate at least three talents. First, we cultivate the capacity to enjoy the body along with God. Just as God enjoys the earth—with its colors, textures, odors, and sounds, and with its varied textures and landscapes—so we, in our way and given our sensory capacities, also enjoy it. Indeed, because God lives in us as well as in other creatures, our eyes become God's eyes, our ears God's ears, our hands, God's hands. Of course, God enjoyed the world before there were humans to enjoy. But to share with humans and with other creatures that capacity to enjoy, and indeed to enjoy our joy, must be one of God's supreme pleasures. As we think of God sharing in our pleasure, we realize that God can appropriately be imaged, not simply as a parent or creator upon whom we are dependent, but as a divine friend and lover: a joyful One who is for us, who desires our happiness on earth, and whose joy is our own.

Second, in seeing the earth as God's body, we cultivate the capacity to heal. We follow the advice of Aldo Leopold, who in proposing his environmental ethic advised that we promote "land health," which is the "capacity of the land for self-renewal."[21] Moreover, we recognize that as we promote land health—that is, the stability and integrity of ecosystems—we promote God's own health. God's own well-being is enriched as we allow a diversity of life forms and land forms to flourish, and as we attempt to preserve the earth from potential dangers which we ourselves might inflict. Often such healing practice involves a capacity simply to let be: to practice non-interference in relation to the earth, allowing its own capacities for growth and self-renewal to flourish in their own right. Sometimes it involves positive action on our part, either to repair previous damage or to aid the earth itself in its growth. Here we practice the healing arts with respect to the earth. We are to God as a physician is to a patient, or a parent is to a child. We nurture the land, and in so doing exercise a tender care for God's body. We allow God to be imaged, not simply as parent, friend, or lover, but as a child, perhaps the baby Jesus. God becomes the Christ child, wrapped in swaddling clothes, whose body is the earth itself, and whose life within that body we seek to nurture and protect with the tender care of parent to child.

Third, in seeing the world as God's body we develop the capacity to accept our own finitude and our dependence on something that ultimately eludes our cognitive grasp. We realize that we, as parts of the earth, are parts of God's body, and hence parts of a cosmic web of interdependence that far transcends our understanding. One of the consequences of participating in this web is finitude. Our own bodies are forms of energy which endure for a time, and then disintegrate, to be succeeded by subsequent forms that are expressions of the very same energy. We are made from the dust of the earth, and we return to it.

Moreover, as we dwell in and from the earth, we sense that we are surrounded by an all-encompassing, womb-like matrix that includes the earth and yet is more than the earth. This entire matrix can be called the totality, the all, or the whole. It is God's body considered in its entirety, including the earth and its mortals, yet also including the celestial sphere of existence, the sky, and the psychological archetypes, the gods. We are never spectators of this totality. Instead, we are within it. It is the universe itself: our home of homes.

## Questions for Reflection and Discussion

1. What environmental problems are most obvious to you in the community in which you live? What is the source of these problems? Who is responsible? What can you do to remedy them?

2. Imagine an "ecological literacy" test that might be used in high schools, colleges and universities. The questions on the test would measure a person's understanding of the earth and its systems and also that person's understanding of the problems the earth faces. What questions would you consider most important for such a test?

3. Compare William Barrett's way of feeling the aliveness of rocks with the way "matter" is generally understood in the natural sciences. Do you find Barrett's perspective compatible with a scientific perspective, or hopelessly romantic compared to scientific perspectives? To what extent do you think the natural sciences now shape our understandings of physical matter?

4. To what extent, and in what ways, do you think an ethic of stewardship, or kindly use, might play a role in capitalism? In socialism? What shape might the theories, institutions, and policies of capitalism and socialism take if these systems took as

their aim the promotion of human community in an ecologically responsible context rather than in the context of ever-increasing production and consumption of material goods?

5. In your experience, how have Christians traditionally thought about the body? Has "the Christian view of the body," as you have experienced it, been constructive or destructive?

6. Do you see any relation between the way the human body—almost always the woman's body—is approached in pornography and the way in which soil is approached in unsustainable agriculture? What ways of thinking about the earth need to emerge in Christianity if Christians are to help overcome both forms of exploitation?

## CHAPTER FIVE

# Openness to the Sky

> In the twilight of
> the twentieth century, scientists themselves are awakening
> at last to the wonder and the mystery of the universe, even
> to its numinous qualities. They are beginning to experience
> also the mythic aspect of their own scientific expressions.
>
> Thomas Berry

Humans cannot live by bread alone. We also need cosmic myths. By "cosmic myths" I do not mean false stories or illusions. Instead, I mean meaningful stories, either symbolically or literally true, about how the universe came into existence and about our place within it. The sky is that which often elicits the quest for such myths. When we gaze into the sky on a starry night, for example, we cannot help but wonder where we have come from and where we are going. Our myths are the products of such wonder.

Today, a new myth concerning the origins of the cosmos is emerging. What is noteworthy is that it is being taught all over the world: in Africa, Asia, Latin America, Oceania, Europe, and North America. But it is not taught by clergy or priests. Rather, it is taught by scientists, in particular, physicists and biologists. It goes something like this:

Some ten to twenty billion years ago all the matter in the universe was condensed into a small concentration of undifferentiated energy. We do not know where this energy came from; in one form or another it may have existed forever. In any case, in a single flash it began to pour into the surrounding nothingness, an event we can call "the big bang" or "the primal flash." One trillionth of a trillionth of a trillionth of a second after the flash, the most elementary units of matter—quarks and leptons, for example—began to materialize, almost like snowflakes crystallizing from a cloud. They began to expand into the surrounding nothingness and to cool. As these elementary units began to fuse, even larger units of matter emerged such as protons and neutrons. At three minutes past zero, the temperature had abated to the degree that compound nuclei, conjunctions of protons and neutrons, materialized. For a long time, at least by human standards, the universe was still too hot for stable atoms to emerge, but after further cooling for about five hundred thousand years, hydrogen and helium atoms did indeed emerge. After even more cooling, stars began to evolve, and galaxies, and, around some stars, planets such as our own.

On our own planet, so the new story continues, life emerged some three and a half billion years ago. The history of life is itself part of a larger cosmic history. This experiment in life has taken myriad forms, both plant and animal, of which we ourselves are instances. There is little if any evidence to suggest that we were the single, appropriate end or aim of evolution; rather, if aims are considered, it seems that there have been many aims. Rattlesnakes and bacteria are as much aims of evolution as are porpoises and humans. In any case, in modern form, our own species emerged some fifty-thousand years ago, though we were preceded by several earlier human-like forms whose roots go back several million years. On other planets, too, there may be something like life, though up to this point we have no direct evidence. All that we know is that we are a fragile yet powerful species on a second-rate planet on the edge of a minor galaxy.

Thus, the new story—now being told around the world—is that of cosmic and biological evolution. Its details may change over time; it may even prove to be utterly false. But for the time being and the foreseeable future, it is the best myth we have. If accepted by religious people, "the new story," as it is called by Thomas Berry, has important implications for overcoming religious prejudices. Despite the fact that heretofore the world's religions have had different myths concerning origins, now we have a common myth.

Indeed, it is a myth that can promote peace. Now all of us— Jewish and Muslim, Hindu and Buddhist, Christian and Marxist—can peer into the heavens on a clear night, gaze at a particular star, and see, in the star itself, a common heritage. For the light that reaches our respective eyes from this distant star was emitted long before its arrival on earth, at a previous stage in the history of the cosmos upon which we are utterly dependent for our existence. Of course, a sense of cosmic history will not itself solve all the problems we face in relation to each other. But it can give us a starting point. (We need as many starting points as we can find.)

Even as they appropriate the new story, however, different religious traditions will have different interpretive lens through which the story is understood. Ecological Christians will see the adventure of evolution in panentheistic terms. They will see cosmic evolution as bearing witness to a divine lure toward self-organization within matter itself, and they will see the countless forms of existence to which evolution gives rise as contributing to a single life, the very God whose body is the universe. When we gaze at the star noted above, we will see the star as part of

God's body, and as an outcome, like us, of the beckoning of the divine spirit.

Still, there is more to the sky than the story of cosmic evolution, important as that story is. Internalizing the new story of cosmic evolution is just one way in which ecological Christians can feel our connectedness with the sky. In the remaining sections of this chapter, let us consider still additional ways.

## Ways of Perceiving the Sky

At the outset it is important to recognize that there can be a tension, and indeed a contradiction, between a spirituality of the sky and one of the earth. Certain skyward spiritualities can lead a person away from the earth and any concern for it. They can encourage other-worldliness and escapism. For this reason, early Christian leaders such as Irenaeus criticized Gnosticism. Irenaeus saw Gnosticism as a world-transcending spirituality that had lost touch with the earth and possibilities for its redemption. Yet a skyward spirituality need not be escapist. The task of this chapter is to describe a spirituality of the sky that might complement rather than contradict a love of the world. To get our bearings, we begin by noting five ways in which the sky can be, and often has been, experienced by humans on earth.

First, it can be experienced as the earth's atmosphere; that is, as the harbinger of weather and bearer of climatic tidings. Sometimes the weather is encouraging and sometimes threatening, which means that sometimes the sky is a friend and sometimes an enemy. In either case, the sky is an actual presence that directly affects life on earth.

Second, the sky can be experienced as the home of moving celestial spheres: the moon, stars and planets. The different spheres can themselves be perceived in different ways. They can be perceived astrologically, that is, as guides of personal life and agents of destiny; religiously, as imaginative depictions of the gods and goddesses; navigationally, as guides for travel; and, as noted above, scientifically, as products of evolution and trans-formers of energy into matter. All of these ways of perceiving are interpretive, as is any form of perception. We see the stars and planets through the lens of constructs and expectations. But we see them nonetheless, and we experience the sky as their home, the receptacle in which their movements occur.

Third, and here we move even more obviously into the area of interpretation, the sky can be experienced as heaven, that is, as a home of God or the gods and goddesses. In the West, this way of experiencing the sky has been characteristic of the three monotheistic traditions: Judaism, Islam, and Christianity; in the East, of Pure Land schools of Buddhism and certain forms of Bhakti Hinduism; in primal traditions, of certain native American perspectives and of African points of view. Just as the sky is above the earth, encompassing it and yet transcending it, so in many traditions God (or at least one of the gods or goddesses) is envisioned as encompassing the earth and yet moving beyond it. God is, as Jesus put it, "Our Father who art in heaven."

A fourth way in which the sky can be experienced, and one that is not unrelated to the one just mentioned, is as a well-spring of possibilities and a spur to the imagination. The God to whom the Hebrew prophets pointed was understood as the pro-vider of new possibilities for action and passion when the peo-ple of Israel and Judah seemed without power or passion.[1] The prophets looked to the sky; that is, to God in Heaven, to discov-er the novum: new and unanticipated possibilities for thought, feeling, and action in this world. God somehow spoke to them from the sky, a voice heard from within—the divine lure—that comes from without. For them, the sky was a reservoir of possi-bilities, a place from which new unexpected possibilities for the earth itself could emerge.

In its capacity as a well-spring of possibilities and spur to the imagination, a fifth way of experiencing the sky emerges. The sky can be experienced as a place of escape from earthly limita-tions, as a place toward which, as the Gnostics recognized in their own ways, the soul ascends in pursuit of mystical union with God. As such, the sky represents the unbounded and un-limited, that domain which has escaped the bondage of flesh and which, in the language of Gnostic traditions, is "spiritual" rather than "material." It reveals possibilities, not for life on earth, but rather for life beyond earth. In this understanding, the sky is again heaven, not simply as God's home, but our own eventual home as well.

As I explore possibilities for a spirituality of the sky, I presup-pose the reality of the sky as atmosphere and home of the stars and planets, and focus on the sky as a home of God, as a well-spring for possibilities for life on earth, and as a well-spring of possibilities for life beyond earth.

## Imaging God in the Sky

Openness to the sky as God's dwelling involves an imaginative leap in which the world is envisioned as a subject of ultimate care: either internally as an object of mental experience, or exter-nally through the senses as represented by maps and globes. This is to conceive the earth from the point of view of the sky, and from the point of view of God, who resides in the sky, at least metaphorically, and for whom the earth is indeed a subject of such care and commitment. Before developing this thesis, however, two questions need to be considered. First, can God be legitimately perceived, albeit imaginatively, as dwelling in the sky? Second, what types of spirituality can emerge in principle from such a perception?

## God in the Sky

For many in the West, the image of God in the sky is oppressive, even when it is recognized that the image is properly under-stood metaphorically rather than literally. The image can carry with it a hierarchical understanding of our relation to God, with humans understood as servile subjects whose meaning comes only through submission to a higher authority. To speak of God as "in the sky" can be to deny human autonomy and freedom; to disallow a growth into adulthood; to foster a psychic disposition of infantile dependency, at least in relation to God. God as thus envisioned—often on the analogy of a parent, and in the West, a father—becomes the one who never allows his children to become adults.

It is no accident that in the twentieth century there has been a revolt against height imagery for the divine, with alternative proposals drawing from depth metaphors. For those who find sky imagery victimizing, God is better conceived as within the self, as many mystical traditions in the West have always stressed, or within the world, as many creation-centered traditions emphasize. Not a few women and men in the twentieth century are more comfortable with God as the underlying ground of being than with God as biblical father in heaven.

For those in this situation, the image of God as father in heaven—or indeed as mother in heaven—may itself never be recoverable. Once the image of God as up and out has become repressive, it can be difficult, if not impossible, to reclaim it as life-nourishing. Fortunately, an inability or unwillingness to experience God as "in heaven" does not prevent a relationship with God. For God is indeed within the psyche as the ever-present call for becoming, and God is indeed in the world, as a divine lure immanent within other creatures as well. God is present wherever we see responsiveness to this lure: in human life, for example, wherever we see openness and care, honesty and creativity, depth and intensity. Those oppressed by sky imagery are quite right to say that God is within the self and within the world, in each instance ever-beckoning for realization.

Yet there are aspects of God that transcend the world, even though we participate in them, and these aspects *can* be imaged as in the sky, if these images are not taken literally and if the imagery is not experienced as oppressive. This way of imaging is justified because, in fact, the visible sky possesses a quality which bears an actual resemblance to God's transcendence. By virtue of this resemblance, the sky can serve as a sacrament of sorts: a visible sign of an invisible grace.

The quality at issue has already been mentioned. It is the sky's presence as an unbounded and encompassing firmament. One way in which God is transcendent is that God, too, is unbounded and encompassing. When we apprehend the sky, we apprehend a reality that in this way has a direct analogy to God. In order to imagine God's unbounded and encompassing love, we can imagine God, among other places, as coextensive with the sky.

## Types of Sky Spirituality

Historically, an imaginative apprehension of God in the sky has given rise to two distinct motifs, two types of spirituality.

The first is that of mystical ascent, one instance of which is the spirituality of the Gnostics.[2] In this motif, we look to the sky as the place where God is, and then we approach the heavens as a place toward which the soul would like to ascend. An instance of such thinking occurs in the Bible, though not in a Gnostic sense, when in Exodus (24:15-18) Moses climbs Sinai in order to receive God's revelations. Here the sky itself is the subject of focus, and the earth is a point of departure. Moses leaves the earth and climbs the mountain in order to approach God.

The second form is quite different. We imagine ourselves as already in the sky, on top of the mountain alongside God, looking back down upon the earth. This is the vantage point in which the writer of Psalm 104 imagines himself when he surveys the wonders of creation and proclaims: "O Lord, how manifold are thy works! In wisdom hast thou made them all; the earth is full of thy creatures." Here the earth is the subject of focus, and the sky is the imaginative perspective from which the earth is viewed. We have left the earth in order to join God, and having joined God, we gaze upon the earth.

Though the two types of sky spirituality are related, they are distinct. Whereas in the spirituality of mystical ascent we are climbing the mountain in order to get to God, perhaps (though not in Moses' instance) to stay there, in this second form we have arrived at the top of the mountain, and we are gazing back at the earth, appreciating its fecundity, along with God, and preparing to descend. This second form can be called "the spirituality of inclusive earth- appreciation," or, when joined with a commitment to the well-being of the earth and its creatures, "world loyalty," to use the phrase of Alfred North Whitehead. In this context I use "world" to refer not to the cosmos as a whole, as I have elsewhere, but to the earth and its living inhabitants.

## World Loyalty

World loyalty depends on a capacity for "putting oneself in the shoes of another," or, as I shall speak of it, *imaginative ego-transcendence*. To imaginatively transcend one's ego is to place oneself in the position of another subject, and to try to perceive the world from that being's point of view. It is to behold the world from a point of view other than that which, normally speaking, one views as one's own.

Typical of ordinary, waking experience as most of us know it is the phenomenon of perceiving the world from "our" point of view, though this point of view continually changes with circumstances. This point of view is defined both by our bodies and by our psychic dispositions, both of which are shaped by biological and social histories. We perceive the world from a point of view defined by our senses and body structure, which are themselves the outcome of distant evolutionary processes, and we respond to the world from the point of view of our own interests, which are shaped by social and historical circumstances. The world "out there" is seen from my point of view "here," where my body is, and "now," at this stage of my life and in light of my concerns.

Imaginative ego-transcendence occurs when we attempt to transcend such limitations. Our attempts are often directed toward one or some combination of three horizons.

First, we sometimes direct our attention to the past. We try to imagine people who lived before us, either in the distant or more recent past, and, as we do so, we try to imagine their lives as lived from their own points of view. We try, if only for a moment, to become our predecessors in our imaginations: to see things as our great-grandmother saw them, hear things as Jesus heard them, feel things as an early hominid felt them. We never fully succeed in these attempts, because our own imaginations are shaped by our social and political circumstances. And sometimes not enough data are available, in which case our acts of imaginative transcendence are largely projective. Whether projective or realistic, however, we momentarily transcend our own perspectives when imagining ourselves in the positions of those who have lived before us.

Second, we sometimes direct our imaginative attention to the present. For example, we often "put ourselves in the shoes of another" in ordinary conversation. Often we do this unconsciously. As someone speaks to us, we try to understand what that person is saying by getting a feel for "where he or she is coming from." To "get a feel for other people" is to recognize that they have needs and concerns of their own; to set aside our own agendas for the moment and thus to listen as they speak from their own points of view, and then to imagine the world from their points of view. Often the imagining is unconscious, occurring concurrently with the listening, and continuously being tested by what is heard. We do it instinctively, or naturally, rather than with deliberate reflection. In so doing, we briefly and gradually transcend our own immediate perspective.

A third instance of imaginative ego-transcendence occurs when we place ourselves inside perspectives belonging to the future. The subjects of imaginative identification can be members of future generations, or they can be contemporaries whose futures will be affected by our present actions. When, for example, we are considering a given course of action, and we ask ourselves how a given action we are considering might affect another person whom we know, we exercise imaginative ego-transcendence in reference to that person's future. We imagine ourselves in the position of that person as he or she might exist in a future that has been affected by that action. We anticipate "how she would feel" or "what she would think" if we performed the action. Clearly such anticipation is at the heart of what is ordinarily called morality. Morality is nourished by an ability to transcend our perspective to some degree, putting ourselves in the position of the other, not simply as the other *has been* and *is*, but as the other *will be* as influenced by our immediate actions. We imagine the other people in their futures, taking on their destinies as parts of our own.

As these examples suggest, imaginative ego-transcendence, even if partial, is important. It is an aid to spirituality, an aid to that process in which we "put on the mind of God" and try to apprehend others as God apprehends them. Just as God is a fellow sufferer who understands each of us from our own points of view, so we, with the help of imaginative ego-transcendence, can become fellow sufferers who understand each other from one another's points of view. We rightly attempt to transcend our own perspectives so as to better include others in our care.

Clearly, the acts of imaginative ego-transcendence described above do not directly involve the sky. In imaginatively placing ourselves in the skins of others, we do not first imagine ourselves in the sky and then descend into their bodies from above. Rather we enter their bodies directly: horizontally rather than vertically. We may sometimes image God as caring from above, but we care from where we stand.

The perspective of the sky becomes relevant when we ask: How many of these "others" do we rightly attempt to include within the scope of our care? It occurs when we ask, as the lawyer asked Jesus, "Who is my neighbor?" (Luke 10:29).

In this context our neighbors are those whom we recognize as having perspectives of their own worthy of our care. They are neighborly, not in the sense of living next door to us, or even in the sense of being friendly to us. Rather, they are neighborly in the sense of being fellow creatures into whose perspectives, at least in principle, we can imaginatively enter and try to understand, so that their well-being can then be sought.

Who, then, are our neighbors? Oftentimes, and wrongly, we limit our neighbors to those with whom we have something in common. We limit them to members of our own family, race, nation, or ideology; we limit them to fellow humans at the expense of other creatures. We forget that, from God's perspective, *all* creatures are, or at least ought to be, neighbors to one another. We forget that we are called by God to love all our neighbors, even our enemies, as God loves them.

And this is where the sky enters. One way to approximate such inclusive love is to imagine ourselves inside God's mind or heart, beholding the world from God's perspective. One way we can imagine this perspective is to imagine ourselves in the sky looking down upon the earth, and caring for all the earth's creatures, each in its particularly and in its relatedness to the other creatures, as does God.

In assuming such an imaginative perspective, we cannot and do not empathize with every creature. There are too many creatures, more than are countable. Yet the imaginative assumption of a divine perspective does allow us to recognize each and every creature as part of a totality of creatures worthy of generalized care. To assume a sky-perspective is to envision plants and animals, including humans, as parts of biotic communities and as participants in that ultimate community which is God's own body. By assuming a perspective in the sky, we can see that totality of creatures with whom, in principle, we can empathize on an individual basis, and we can recognize that totality of creatures—that family—which merits our commitment. Imagining ourselves in the sky helps us to be clear about who, in fact, our neighbors are.

This imaginative act is not all that extraordinary. We partially perform this act every time we look at a world map, a world globe, or a photograph of the earth. As we look at the representation of the earth, we imaginatively stand above the earth and its inhabitants, gazing at them from afar. Implicitly, we look at the map from the point of view of the sky. And, indeed, it is just such a perspective that is necessary if we are to be globally conscious. With the help of maps, globes, and photographs, we briefly stand outside the earth, so that we behold the earth as our home, cognizant of the fact that we exist amid a totality of interrelated creatures. Maps, globes, and photographs are our mandalas for an act of imaginative ego-transcendence.

But the act of imaginative ego-transcendence with the help of maps, globes, and photographs is only partial if it stops at mere beholding. The key to genuine openness is not simply to try, as best one can, to behold the world as a totality of living beings inhabiting a small planet in a backwater galaxy. Rather, the key is to care for the world in its totality; that is, to behold the world with an inward sense of affection for its creatures, oneself included, and to desire the indivisible salvation—the well-being— of all those creatures.

Such ego-transcendence is rightly accompanied by a personal capacity for self-relativization. Seeing the world as a totality, we relativize our individual perspectives as North and South Americans, or Africans, or Indians, recognizing that these perspectives are limited and shaped by context. We appreciate that there are other earthly perspectives which also have beauty and value. Moreover, in light of our knowledge of evolution and the history of life on earth, we relativize the time in which we live. We recognize that our historical epoch, too, is one among many, meriting no claim to finality. We see that even our most deeply-held convictions have been historically conditioned, and that they are part of a larger history of life on earth, which itself is part of a larger history of the cosmos.

The "self" that is relativized amid self-relativization is that self which stands on the earth, not in the sky, and that proceeds from a limited perspective, not an unlimited one. Each of us is a self of this sort, even as we imagine ourselves outside ourselves. It is this finite self that does the imagining, and in so doing assumes the task of taking on the joys and the sufferings of the world.

Its capacities to do so are limited in at least two ways. In the first place, we are sometimes unable to understand the joys of others, because our contexts are too different and our imaginations too limited. Taking on the joys of others involves a magnanimity and humility, for we recognize that not all joys are ours to directly experience. In relation to fellow humans, for example, if we are Christians we may not know what the Buddhist experiences in nirvana, but we celebrate the fact that nirvana is experienced; we may not know what the Muslim experiences in pilgrimage to Mecca, but we celebrate the fact that the pilgrimage can be taken; we may not know what the Vedantist experiences in Brahmanic absorption, but we celebrate the fact that *sat-chit-ananda* has been realized. When we are open to the sky as God's home, the joys of others are ours to affirm from afar—that is, from that divine perspective we imaginatively assume, a perspective in which diversity is celebrated in its own right—but these joys are not ours to experience from within.

In our inability to fully share in other's joys, we differ from God even as we imagine ourselves sharing God's point of view. For God experiences these joys not only from afar, but also from within. In God's empathy, each joy is known and understood on its own terms, in its own right. Given our finitude, we recognize that, even in our noblest attempts to be open to others, our own projections intervene.

A second way in which we are limited, even as we imagine ourselves sharing God's point of view, is in our capacity to share in the sufferings of others. Sometimes our own sufferings are too great, and we cannot bear the additional burdens. Those suffering from hunger and malnutrition, or from torture and repression, or from other forms of deep personal tragedy, cannot be expected to take on the sufferings of others. Their sufferings are quite enough. Moreover, those of us in the advantaged classes cannot take on the sufferings of others simply because we do not fully understand. Because of our own contexts, we do not fully know what it is like to suffer hunger or malnutrition, or political torture, or certain forms of personal tragedy. It is arrogant to pretend otherwise. An inclusive earth-appreciation—a world loyalty—is noble in the scope of its intentions, yet humble in its claims to a fulfillment of these intentions. With Jesus, it recognizes that "only God is good," only God exemplifies *unlimited* empathy.

Nevertheless, when a capacity for self-relativization is combined with an inward sense of affection for all the earth's creatures, we have a form of spirituality that is worthy of our embodiment. Recognizing the world as a network of interdependent creatures, a network in which the spiritual "self" is itself included, this spirituality takes on the world's destiny as its own. In the latter sense it is "loyal" to the world, which is to say that it is a form of world loyalty. Such loyalty is always partial. We never fully approximate that appreciation of the world, and loyalty to the world, which is characteristic of God. God's fidelity to the world, exercised through empathy and invitation, is stronger than the world's to itself. Furthermore, world loyalty, even when approximated to a high degree, is by no means sufficient for a complete spirituality. It must always be complemented by an ability to attend to, and care for, particular creatures as particular creatures. Yet such loyalty is by all means necessary for a complete, holistic spirituality. If we are to love the world as God loves it, we must love the *whole* world as best we can. It is the presence of the sky, and our imaginative entrance into its point of view, that allows us to love the world in this way.

## The Sky as a Stimulus for Earthly Hope

We cannot stay on the mountain forever. A full-fledged spirituality of the sky involves more than openness to the sky as God's home. It involves more than seeing the sky as a vantage point from which God cares about the whole world, and into which we might imaginatively enter. Sky spirituality also includes, as mentioned earlier, openness to the sky as a well-spring of possibilities for life on earth. It includes, not only a beholding the earth from the point of view of the sky, but also beholding the sky from the point of view of the earth. Here the sky is not a vantage point from which the earth is imaginatively beheld, rather it is a resource for imagining how things can and should be in the world, in contrast to how they are.

Such openness corresponds to the fourth way of experiencing the sky described earlier, to what Walter Brueggemann calls "the prophetic imagination." This is the imagination—the consciousness—of the Hebrew prophets, of Jesus, and of prophetic people today. It is a consciousness that has opened itself to possibilities for criticizing the principalities and powers of a given society when they are oppressive and unjust, and for energizing the victimized to have hope amid their victimization. Brueggemann points out how Moses, Jeremiah, Isaiah, and Jesus exemplified this mode of consciousness, either criticizing the authorities of their time, energizing the outcasts and disenfranchised, or both. He proposes that contemporary ministers do the same: "The task of prophetic ministry is to nurture, nourish, and evoke a consciousness and perception alternative to the consciousness and perception of the dominant culture around us."[3] To do so, he explains, a minister must be open to the novum, that is, to the presence of new and unanticipated possibilities for thought, feeling, and action derived, unasked for, from God in heaven.

The sky need not be called heaven, or for that matter be associated with God, in order to function as a resource for the prophetic imagination. Consider the case of science fiction. Most of this literature is non-theological, and the sky has been freed of the suggestion that it is God's home. Nevertheless, in much science fiction the sky functions as a resource for imagining what is possible, for what *can be* in contrast to what *is*.

More specifically, the sky inspires the writer to imagine possible worlds beyond this one: worlds in which beings both resemble and differ from terrestrial forms of life. Though unearthly, these imagined worlds are not unreal. Rather, they are real as *possibilities*, as items apprehended in the imagination rather than as items apprehended through sense perception. Furthermore, just as the sky-inspired possibilities discovered by the Hebrew prophets came from the sky, and yet were relevant to the earth, so the sky-inspired possibilities discovered by science fiction writers can be relevant to the earth. As Sallie McFague writes in reference to one science fiction writer, Ursula LeGuin:

> When a fantasy writer asks, "What if things were very different from the way we are accustomed to seeing them?," she is asking a serious question. Speculative fiction is not necessarily frivolous or unrelated to "reality."... One of the most powerful ways to question a tradition is to imagine new worlds that challenge it. Speculative fiction, with more tenuous ties to everyday life than "realistic" fiction, creates a world in sharp contrast to our conventional one, and hence, simply by juxtaposition questions and criticizes it.[4]

For science fiction writers such as LeGuin, so McFague explains, the sky points not only beyond the earth, toward what is possible, but also to the earth, toward what can and should be, but is not. Indirectly, the sky reveals possibilities for life on earth.

As the example of LeGuin's science fiction attests, even when the sky is not called heaven and not associated with God, it can serve as a stimulus for that prophetic imagination which is in fact responsive to God. Wherever there is openness to the sky as resource for possibilities for life on earth, there is, consciously or unconsciously, openness to God. In such instances, openness takes the form of the prophetic or eschatological imagination: an imagining of the way things can be and ought to be on earth, in contrast to the way things are. By imagining other worlds located in the sky, such imagining attends to the will of God as it is done in heaven. Then it hopes, like Jesus, that this will can also be done on earth. Science fiction writers on the one hand, and biblical prophets on the other, can each exhibit such imagination. Their piety of prophetic hope holds an important place in an ecological spirituality.

## The Sky as a Stimulus for Heavenly Hope

Openness to the sky as just described is one way of being open to the future and to the beckoning of God. In and through imaginative possibilities evoked by a prophet's awareness of the heavens, we are open to hopeful possibilities for the improvement of life on earth. Such openness—the prophet's and our own—is eschatological in the sense that it involves the anticipation, not of a final end, but rather of provisional ends for which we realistically hope, and toward which we rightly strive.

As discussed in the first chapter, it is important for us to be realistic about our hopes for life on earth. In that chapter I identified our best hope as a state of affairs in which maximum degrees of social justice, ecological sustainability, and spiritual satisfaction are realized. Even if this best hope is realized, we would have to recognize, first, that its actualization will be impermanent. At some point in the indefinite future, life on earth will cease. Second, amid its actualization, there will still be pain, tragedy, disease, and, in the natural order, violence. As long as we eat, cut down trees, kill cancer cells, or wash germs from our hands and faces, we will be participating in that robbery of life which is, like it or not, essential to life on earth as we know it. We will be taking the lives of creatures whose will it is to live.

Moreover, there will be hardships and heartaches in the human order: lost loves, failed friendships, untimely deaths, debilitating diseases. Even if our best hope is realized, we will not have that complete peace, that freedom from all disease, tension, and violence, for which at a deep level, for ourselves and for others, our hearts may long.

The longing of the heart for a complete peace points to a second kind of eschatological hope: a hope for ultimate fulfillment to be attained in some other world after death. If in the previous section our subject was the sky as a source for terrestrial eschatology, our subject here is the sky as a source for other-worldly eschatology.

That the sky can function as a source for other-worldly hopes is evident not only in traditional images of heaven, where the end of human existence is conceived as occuring in a other-worldly place, but also in those forms of science fiction, such as Arthur Clarke's *2001: A Space Odyssey*, which celebrate space travel as the last and final frontier of human fulfillment. In both instances, the sky invites humans to imagine non-earthly worlds in which fulfillment—indeed ultimate and unsurpassable fulfillment—can be obtained. The question we must ask is this: Can these kinds of hopes, or some versions thereof, be affirmed within the purview of an ecological spirituality?

Some would say, of course, that longing for complete peace is itself a disease, a failure to accept finitude. Our best hopes are enough, they would say; we need not ask for more. Others would say that complete peace can in fact be obtained, but only in life as we know it through an inner acceptance of uncontrollable earthly circumstances. Completion is not the conformation of earthly reality to our ideals, so they would argue, but rather the relinquishment of ideals through an acceptance of unmanipulable earthly realities.

There is truth in each of these critiques. If the longing for perfect peace involves an avoidance of finitude, then such peace is escapist; and if this longing involves an excessive molding of reality to private purposes, such peace is imperialistic. The general point is this: If hopes for life beyond earth are indulged at the expense of an appreciation of the earth and its creatures, then other-worldly hopes cannot be reconciled with this-worldly concerns. To the question, "Can trans-terrestrial hopes be affirmed within the purview of an ecological spirituality?" the answer would be "no," because such hopes would contradict that world loyalty—that openness to plants, animals, fellow humans, and the earth itself—which is essential to an ecological worldview. Those of us in search of a holistic spirituality would then have to choose *between* a spirituality of the earth and a spirituality of the sky as the latter is expressed in heavenly eschatologies. Out of world loyalty, most of us would choose the earth.

I suggest, however, that some versions of other-worldly hope can be appropriated within an ecological or relational perspective. Some forms of hope for life beyond earth can be understood as extensions of, rather than obstacles to, world loyalty.

If, for example, it becomes clear that human survival depends on space colonization, then clearly a hope for this form of life beyond earth will complement, not contradict, world loyalty. Furthermore, the very adventure of space exploration and colonization can be perceived as an extension of that exploratory impulse by which life on earth is enriched and enhanced. If they are complemented by this-worldly social concerns, space exploration and colonization can be understood as legitimate hopes for the human enterprise. Those interested in these possibilities may be responding to one aspect of the divine lure.

Moreover, the sheer enjoyment of imagining what lies in the celestial beyond—of imagining what is in the heavens, and what is not—can be a legitimate form of spirituality in its own right. The possibilities thus imagined, often well articulated by science fiction novelists, need not be possibilities *for us* in order to be enjoyed by us as imaginative objects in their own right. Our consideration of them can be one way in which we recognize our own finitude, our own limitations, in light of the unknown, and it can be one way in which, perhaps, we are linked with whatever forms of life might inhabit the celestial regions. Imagination, like prayer, can establish connections not accessible to the senses.

However, the form of trans-earthly hope, on which I focus in closing this chapter, is that "ultimate hope" mentioned above. I shall call it the "hope for heaven." For those of us in comfortable situations, this hope takes its most profound form, not when we entertain it for ourselves, but rather when we entertain it for others, particularly those who die in tragedy. Here the hope for heaven emerges, not out of a failure to accept our own finitude, but rather out of desire that others—who, too, are finite—find fulfillment amid their finitude.

Consider the case of the young boy whose death by hanging in a Nazi concentration camp is described so vividly by Elie Wiesel in *Night*.[5] After being tortured, the boy is being hanged along with two adults for suspicion of insubordination.

> The three necks were placed at the same moment within the nooses.
> "Long live liberty!" cried the two adults.
> But the child was silent.
> "Where is God? Where is He?" someone behind me asked.
> At the sign from the head of the camp, the three chairs tipped over.
> Total silence throughout the camp. On the horizon the sun was setting.
> Then the march past began. The two adults were no longer alive. Their tongues hung swollen, blue-tinged. But the third rope was still moving; being so light, the child was still alive....
> For more than half an hour he stayed there, struggling between life and death, dying in slow agony under our eyes. And we had to look him full in the face. He was still

alive when I passed in front of him. His tongue was still red, his eyes were not yet glazed.

Behind me, I heard the same man asking: "Where is God now?" And I heard a voice within me answer him: "Where is He? He is hanging here on this gallows...."

That night the soup tasted of corpses.[6]

From the point of view of a relational spirituality, in which God, too, is relational, and therefore influenced and affected by the world's sufferings, Wiesel was correct: God *was* hanging there on the gallows. Wherever there are crosses, they belong to God, for inasmuch as the world is God's body, whatever happens in the world happens to God. But this recognition of divine suffering does not alleviate our concern for the boy. The question is: Was there—is there—any hope for this boy?

Clearly, when hanging on the gallows, there was no hope for him on earth. His last moments were spent gasping in pain. And these painful moments were not compensated by prior moments of joy. As a young victim of the Holocaust, he was born into tragedy, he lived in tragedy, and he died in tragedy. And he was not alone. He represents countless persons and other animals who have suffered such fates. Is there hope for those whose lives have been a bagatelle of suffering, despair, and pain?

Note that such a question comes not from a neglect of life on earth, but rather from an appreciation of it. It emerges out of a belief that life on earth can and should be good: that is, experientially rich with, in the case of humans, friendships, personal achievements, spiritual depth, and care for others. We ask the question because we bemoan the fact that so many have not been able to enjoy this richness of experience. In addition, the question emerges because we recognize that there can be *good* deaths, that is, deaths that are peaceful, imbued with a sense of completeness, a sense of having had, and completed, a rich and full life. We ask the question of whether there is hope for the boy and for all whose lives are full of tragedy, because we want for them good lives and good deaths.

Nevertheless, there may not be any hope for the boy. It may be that the boy's entire existence was exhausted by his few years of pain, and that, at least for him and so many others, life is unfair.

I believe, however, that it is possible and acceptable for us to hope that his death on the gallows was not his last moment. We can hope that his life continued in some way, in some other plane of existence, not necessarily indefinitely, but rather until he, too, had some opportunity for a good life and a good death. This is not to hope that he or anybody else lives forever, but rather to hope that he lived until some sense of satisfaction could be realized. The satisfaction obtained would be relative to his needs and desires, and it would take into account, though not erase, the tragedy of his past. It may well involve a reunion with loved ones from whom, in life, he was separated.

This is not the time or place to go into whether, on cosmological or metaphysical grounds, such a hope can be legitimated. To entertain such a hope is to suppose that 1) the human (or animal) psyche is in some sense different from the body; 2) a psyche can survive bodily death; 3) there are planes of existence other than the four-dimensional plane in which such survival might take place; and 4) that in these planes there could be interaction between psyches. It is also to suppose that the divine lure would be available to psyches after life on earth, such that they could grow toward wholeness, just as it is available to psyches during life on earth.

The idea of growth after death can even open the door for a doctrine of hell. For those who have harmed others, and here we are all included, the growth toward wholeness might involve empathy with, and thus understanding of, those, both human and nonhuman, whom we have victimized. We would then share in the very suffering for which we are responsible. Such empathy would be its own kind of hell, yet would also lead to reconciliation. Hell would be a temporary stage on the way to wholeness, a purgation leading, it is hoped, to heavenly reconciliation.

But can such suppositions be legitimated? Under the rubric of subjective immortality, process theologians have argued, and I think persuasively, that life after death, as understood above, is a metaphysical possibility. Whether or not it is an actuality is a matter not to be known, if at all, until after death itself. Christians informed by the events of the resurrection can only hope that that which is left so unreconciled in this life can be reconciled in life after death.

The point to be underscored is that such hope need not contradict a deep concern with life on earth. Rather, it can issue from world loyalty, out of a conviction that life can and should be good. Indeed, it can issue out of a conviction that death, too, can be good. What is hoped for in life after death is not that finitude be escaped, but rather that it be completed.

And what occurs after this completion of the life process? Here we can learn from Hinduism, from the idea that what is most desirable is not the indefinite continuation of separate beings, but rather the absorption of all beings into the life of God. This absorption would be both the satisfactory completion and cessation of personal existence. It is a death which is life, a death in which one's life becomes absorbed into God's life. Such is the deepest meaning of heaven. It is that perfect peace for which the heart yearns.

Christians embodying an ecological spirituality can hope, albeit with humility and tentativeness, that all sentient beings will in some way complete their journeys, living out individual existence to its fullest, and then dying to themselves, joining God in heaven. Feeling this hope, and allowing it to well within our hearts, is one way we can be open to the sky even as we feel solidarity with the earth.

# Questions for Reflection and Discussion

1. Imagine that the universe is in its original state prior to the big bang, and that a big bang is going to occur all over again. The initial conditions for this second big bang would be utterly identical to the initial conditions. From the point of view of this work, would the events that have occured this time around necessarily occur again? Would the planet earth necessarily evolve again, and would we, along with other creatures, necessarily inhabit this planet? Would you necessarily be reading this question a second time around? Your answer might be enhanced by referring to the notions of emptiness and God as introduced in Chapter Two.

2. To what extent do you find it helpful, and to what extent oppressive, to imagine God in the sky? Is a God who is "in the sky" necessarily authoritarian in the negative sense of the word? Is such a God necessarily more masculine than feminine? Explain your answer.

3. This chapter proposes that the sky is a stimulus to hope for new and better futures on earth. Review the suggestion that science fiction, in which openness to the sky stimulates an awareness of "what can be" in contrast to "what is," can sometimes aid in the cultivation of such hope. Identify some works in science fiction which in your view substantiate this claim. Identify some works, on the other hand, which seem escapist rather than hope-inspiring. What is the difference between these two types of works?

4. Review the concept of world loyalty. In your view, is this idea relevant to people who are poor and powerless, or only to people who are privileged and powerful? Is it relevant to people who are struggling for a sense of national self-identity, such as many people in the Third World, or is it relevant only to people who already enjoy such identity? Explain your answers.

5. An ecological spirituality aims to respect diversity through the cultivation of imaginative ego-transcendence. Review the latter concept and discuss its possible application to solving problems of racism, sexism, and anthropocentrism. How might education be transformed to help us cultivate our own capacities for such transcendence?

6. Review the concept of hell articulated in this chapter. Do you find it agreeable or disagreeable? Explain your response.

7. In your view, is the hope for life after death compatible with socially responsible hopes for a more just and sustainable world? Explain your answer.

## CHAPTER SIX

# Openness
to the Gods

A Native American boy claimed that during a thunderstorm he saw a thunderbird. Some among his tribe were skeptical, since to see a thunderbird in such fashion, that is, with the waking eye, was almost unheard of. One of the elders was approached. "Was it a real thunderbird?" the skeptics asked. "Yes," said the man. "I have seen thunderbirds in dreams, and the boy's description matches my dream. He has seen a thunderbird." The boy's seeing of the thunderbird was verified.[1]

There is something strange about this episode. Ordinarily, if influenced by modern Western ways of thinking, we do not often think of dream experience as a source for verifying perceptions in the physical world. "You can't verify a person's perception of something by appeal to a dream," we might say, "for dreams are fictional; they reveal nothing real!"

But not so for most Native American cultures, where, as J. Baird Callicott explains, dreams often have a "higher degree of truth than ordinary waking experiences, since in dream experiences the person and everything he meets is present in spirit, in essential self."[2] The dream world is part of the larger social environment in which a person lives, and there is as much to be learned from dreams as there is to be learned from the physical environment and other people. It is not simply a world *projected* by the individual's psyche, it is a world the individual *discovers* through dream experience. The dream world is as real in its own way as is the physical world in its way.

An ecological spirituality will agree with the Native Americans in this regard. It will recognize that the range of existence includes the invisible as well as the visible, the psychic as well as the physical, the imagistic as well as the material. By "the imagistic" I mean the entire realm of internal images present to us in dreams, fantasies, prayer, worship, and other modes of consciousness. These images are "internal" in the sense that they are seen with our mind's eye, our imagination, rather than with our physical eyes. But they are not necessarily unreal. We do not simply produce them, as if they had no reality apart from our conscious egos; rather, at least in part, they come to us, revealing worlds of their own. The faculty by which we discern them can be called "the imagination," but it is important to recognize that "the imagination" is as much receptive as it is generative. It is like a sixth sense. It receives transmissions from other worlds, whether domains of the human subconscious or planes of existence in their own right, and it then interprets these images in light of the interests, needs, and social circumstances of the imaginer. Images are not simply produced by the imagination; they come to it.

In affirming the world of internal images and the capacities of the human imagination an ecological spirituality will be "open to the gods." The gods—or, better, the gods and goddesses—are one type of internal image that can present itself to the imagination. They are those internal images—whether faces or voices, human-like or animal-like, terrestrial or cosmic—that are experienced by the imaginer herself as revelatory of the divine. Such images need not be "seen" in the mind's eye; instead, they can be "felt" or "heard" or in some other way "touched." And they are not necessarily clear or distinct in their self-disclosure; more often than not they are dim and vague, in the background rather than in the foreground of consciousness. In any case they are "real" inasmuch as they exercise a powerful influence in our lives and inasmuch as they can, if we are open, guide us into richer connections with the earth, the sky, and other mortals. Of course, some gods or goddesses—those that beckon us toward violence or self-hatred—can be dangerous and oppressive. We rightly recognize them as inhabitants of our psyches, but we also rightly resist their promptings. At the end of this chapter I propose a criterion by which we, as Christians, might evaluate gods and goddesses. For now, however, let us turn to that god by whom many of us in Christianity have been most deeply shaped for good or ill: the internal image of a "father in heaven." For it is only in recognizing that "the father," too, is an image among images, a god among gods, that we can understand why it might be important to open ourselves to other images as well.

## God the Father

"Our father, who art in heaven" is an imagistic presence who has had a profound impact on Western civilization. Even if at a conceptual level we insist that we do not really think of divine as a "father" because we know that "he" has no gender, we may nevertheless feel, in the recesses of our own subconsciousness, that the divine is somehow a male presence. When we pray, we pray to "him" rather than "her," and we feel like "he" is listening to us as a fatherly presence. Such is the impact that the *image* of a divine father has had on Christian consciousness. Indeed, it is difficult for many even to use the word "God" without imagining, somewhere in the back of our consciousness, a fatherly presence.

This fatherly presence can be and has been experienced in many ways, not all of which are meaningful for an ecological spirituality. For example, the divine father can be experienced as a cosmic policeman, the very thought of whom elicits fear of eternal damnation; or as an all-determining puppeteer, who causes or permits everything to happen in the world just as it does, including the tragedies suffered by people, other animals, and the earth; or as an ever-present authority who demands intellectual obedience at the expense of mature doubt. None of these ways of experiencing "the father" are particularly conducive to an ecological spirituality. Indeed, the image of a divine father is particularly pernicious when combined, as it has been in the Christian tradition, with the image of a divine king. Then the father becomes a political monarch who "lords over" the world, and who, at least as interpreted by true believers, invites men to "lord over" women and humans to "lord over" the earth and other animals. This monarchical image of the divine is quite problematic from the vantage point of an ecological spirituality.

Nevertheless, there are at least three ways in which "God the father" has been, and can be, experienced that can complement an ecological faith.

First, the divine father can be experienced as a dimly discerned, imaginatively apprehended loving parent who watches over us with a tender care. Even here, of course, there are problems. For many of us who are white and who live in the West, this cosmic parent first appeared in childhood as it did to Michelangelo when he painted the Sistine Chapel, as an old and powerful, bearded white male. The image of a white god can easily sanction racism; just as the image of a male god can sanction sexism. But if we are careful to avoid these liabilities, the image of a "cosmic parent" called "our heavenly father" can still be healing. We can recognize that, after all, the divine father is truly a spirit, that literally speaking "he" has no face, and that his whiteness, and perhaps his exclusive maleness, were largely our own projection. "Our heavenly father" can then be experienced as a dim, vaporous presence: a "fatherly" spirit who watches over us "from above" and cares for us and for all living beings. Inasmuch as an ecological spirituality does indeed model the divine Mystery as a cosmic Psyche who cares for all creatures and for the cosmos as a whole, and inasmuch as such a spirituality recognizes that, under certain circumstances and if not taken too literally, the Mystery can be imagined as encompassing the earth much as the sky encompasses the earth, the image of a tender "father who art in heaven"—if rid of its liabilities—can indeed enrich an ecological spirituality.

The second way in which the image of a divine father can be experienced, and which, too, can complement an ecological spirituality, is as an inner beckoning, a still small voice. Here, too, we are talking about images, but not visual images. Rather, we are talking about auditory images, the image of a "calling" presence within us whom we hear, or perhaps better *feel*, within our own consciousness. In different contexts we may experience the "father's voice" as calling us to love life, to accept death, to appreciate beauty, to seek truth, to work for justice, to care for the earth, to love others, and to love ourselves. If this voice is consistent with the ideals of shalom, the "father's voice" can be a medium through which we experience the lure of the Mystery, the lure toward shalom. Thus understood, the father is the object—or, better, the subject—of the "faith without absolutes" discussed in the second chapter.

The third way in which the divine father can be experienced is as a womb-like receptacle of our own experiences and actions. Here "our father" is one who hears our prayers, who suffers with our sufferings, who shares our joys, and who is affected by our destinies. "Our father" is a medium through which we recognize the Mystery as that cosmic heart whose very body is the universe. "He" is one who is moved to pity by our sufferings and by the sufferings of each and every living being, and whose very life is deeply connected with our own. Here the divine father is a lens through whom the receptive side of the Mystery, the divine Psyche, is experienced. This way of experiencing the divine father, too, can enrich an ecological spirituality, particularly if it is emphasized that the father shares in the joys and sufferings of all living beings, not humans alone.

Thus "God the Father" can be experienced 1) as cosmic person watching over us, and all living beings, with tender care, 2) as a call within us beckoning us toward the fullness of life for ourselves and others, and 3) as an empathetic receiver of our joys and sufferings, and those of each and every living being as well. In each instance "he" is a divine presence, a living image, by whom we are influenced and, in the third instance, whom we ourselves influence. He is an agent and a patient, a giver and a receiver, a speaker and a hearer, a power and a receptacle. He is "our father who art in heaven."

Important as this presence has been in the history of Western religion, and meaningful as it can be to some who seek an ecological spirituality, however, a study of world religions makes us realize that this divine father is by no means the only imaginal presence through whom the Mystery can be experienced. A study of world religions shows us, for example, that there have been female faces and voices through whom the Mystery has been felt: from Ishtar of the ancient Near East through Demeter of ancient Greece and Durga of India to Hathor of ancient Egypt and Kuanyin of China. The Mystery has been imaged as a goddess as well as a god, and, as goddess, the Mystery has also disclosed divine tenderness and power. In many ways the goddess, envisioned as terrestrial or cosmic, has better revealed the Mystery's connection with the earth and other living beings than has "God the Father," particularly when the latter has been conceived supernaturalistically rather than panentheistically (see Chapter Two).

Moreover, we learn from the history of religion there have been many non-white, non-Western faces through whom the Divine has been felt: from Mani of North America through Mulungu of East Africa to Amida of Japan and Vishnu of India. Are not these, too, imaginally apprehended presences through whom people have touched the Mystery? Cannot these, too, be resources for an ecological spirituality? What stance should Christians take toward these other gods and goddesses? Should we, in fact, be open to gods and goddesses beyond "our heavenly father"? I believe we should. In addition to the fact that an exclusive fidelity to the image of a heavenly father has often sanctioned racism and sexism, there are three reasons why Christians should open themselves to new imagery.

## Beyond "God the Father"

First, of course, is the simple fact that many Christians need and desire alternative images to a heavenly father for their own personal piety. Inasmuch as this father has often been pictured as white, Christians of color in Asia, Africa, and Latin America rightly yearn for images of the Divine—to present to their children and to appropriate themselves in a symbolic way—that affirm who they are in their gender and races, their cultural traditions and their heritages, their joys and their sufferings. If, as is so often the case in the education of children, images are to be used, the need is for a black or brown god, not a white one, even if, later, such imagery is itself is left behind. Furthermore, inasmuch as the heavenly father is analogous to a male, many woman, and some men as well, are left out. They cannot identify with a male god in whose name, as tradition has had it, women and the earth have been denigrated. Here, again, there is need for alternative images.

The second reason why it is desirable to explore images beyond the heavenly father has to do with our increasing awareness of the variety of world religions, and our concomitant recognition that, even if there is in fact one divine reality, there are many different ways in which that reality can be imaged. In the words of John Hick, "God has many names," and "God" is but one of many such names.[3] If we are to enter into dialogue with other religions, we must be conscious of, and sensitive to, the many different names of the Divine, each of which represent different faces and aspects of the cosmic Mystery.

Consider, for example, what we might learn from Hindu gods and goddesses. To learn about the Divine as Krishna—the playful boy-god of Hinduism who cavorts with his lover Radha—can be to learn something about the Mystery that would not be learned by limiting one's prayers to a cosmic parent. The more we reflect upon the Divine as Krishna, the more we see that the Mystery has a playful dimension, and that this playful dimension is connected with human sexuality. To learn about God as Kali—the dark goddess whose dishevelled hair, necklace of severed human heads, and blood-dripping mouth frighten even the most bold—can be to learn something about the Mystery that would not be learned by limiting one's prayers to a heavenly father. Through Kali we see that the Mystery's goodness somehow transcends the sentimental goodness of human convention, and that amid this goodness there is a power that is awesome in comparison to human power. And to learn about the Divine as Shiva—more particularly, as the androgynous Shiva whose icons depict a male on one side of the body and a female on the other—and then to meditate upon this androgynous spirit, can be to recognize something about the Mystery that would not be learned by praying to a fatherly co-sufferer. We can see the androgynous character of the Divine, seeing that it includes and transcends rigidly compartmentalized sexual stereotypes. The divine Mystery is not simply beyond maleness and femaleness, as if they were something to be transcended; it is inclusive of maleness and femaleness, containing within itself the fullness of sexual mystery.

Of course, some of these insights can be gained by mining

riches from our own tradition. This is to be celebrated. Yet the insights need not be gained in this fashion. Committed as it is to the idea that wherever there is truth there is the spirit of God, an ecological spirituality can freely draw upon other heritages as well. Christ is, after all, a Way that excludes no ways.

The third reason why such openness to various gods and goddesses can be recommended pertains less to the divine Mystery and more to the polymorphous character of the human psyche. As we become more and more aware of the cultural and biological plurality of our world, we also become more and more aware of the plurality within ourselves, within our own psyches. From season to season, day to day, and sometimes hour to hour, we live and breathe in different moods, different styles, different subjective worlds. This diversity can be desirable; it can enrich that well-being toward which the Mystery calls us. Rigid monotheism sometimes obstructs a respect for psychic diversity by attempting to evaluate all different styles of consciousness, in ourselves and in others, in terms of a single, all-encompassing norm, understood as the will of a monotheistic deity. What is needed is respect for psychic diversity. This respect can be cultivated through an internalization of what can be called "the polytheistic consciousness." Here the gods and goddesses are understood as psychological archetypes around which patterns of human consciousness and behavior are centered. In this context as well, an ecological Christian spirituality can be open to the gods and goddesses.

In order for us to be open to these gods, however, we must first be convinced that, in some sense, they are real. Are they?

## The Reality of Other Gods and Goddesses

Whether Demeter, Shiva, Krishna, Hathor, Kali, and other gods and goddesses are real depends, of course, on how we understand the word "real." Two possible meanings come to mind.

First (and this is the understanding of "real" mentioned in

the introduction to this chapter), something is "real" if it can exercise a powerful influence on us quite apart from the conscious designs of our own egos. Clearly in this sense the gods and goddesses are real, at least for those who are affected by them. Just as dream images have lives of their own from the point of view of the the dreamer, so, for those who experience and are influenced by them, the gods and goddesses have lives of their own from the point of view of those they influence. And, like dream images, these divine presences are not mere two-dimensional photographs devoid of agency; rather they are three-dimensional holograms with agency and patience of their own. From an experiential point of view, the gods and goddesses speak, and we listen; we pray, and they hear. Of course, most Christians have always experienced "the father" as real in this sense. The point here is that other gods and goddesses have this kind of reality as well. All living gods and goddesses have, for those in whom they live, independence from the conscious ego. They have what we can call experiential reality.

Second, (and this is what many people mean by "real"), something can be called "real" if it is capable of existing in partial independence from human experience, including subconscious experience. This can be called ontological reality: the reality something has as a being in its own right. If the gods or goddesses are real in this sense, then they exist in some plane of reality other than the human plane, and they would thus exist even if there were not humans to behold them. Many Christians have assumed that "the heavenly father" is real in this sense. The question is: might not other gods and goddesses also be real in this sense?

It is interesting that the early biblical authors seem to have assumed that they did have such reality. For these earliest authors there were other gods in addition to Yahweh. It took centuries for the people of Israel to decide that Yawheh, who was subsequently imaged as "our father who art in heaven," was the only actual god. Monotheism, in which one and only one sacred power is affirmed, was itself the product of an evolution in belief and sensibility.

The ecological spirituality I have been proposing in this work is in fact monotheistic. It accepts the view, which itself evolved over time, that there is a single, ultimate Mystery to which we give our deepest trust, by which we can be guided, and through which all things are held together in tender care. This does not mean, however, that ecological Christians must necessarily deny the ontological reality of gods and goddesses. It is *possible* that gods and goddesses exist as intra-terrestrial or extra-terrestrial spirits, wraithlike entities analogous to what the Bible calls "angels of the Lord," through whom, in certain circumstances, the Mystery is revealed. Though it is not fashionable for modern, scientifically-influenced people to think this way, it is by no means clear that the modern fashion is the final word. Reality itself may be more complex and multi-faceted than meets the scientific eye, and it may indeed include a "world of spirits," as the vast majority of humans on the planet have traditionally believed. If what people have experienced as "the gods and goddesses," and here I would include god the father, are ontologically real, these spirits would be creatures with thought and feeling something like our own, though in some instances existing in dimensions other than our own. And yet they would be objects—or better, subjects—through whom, at times, the divine Mystery would be revealed. At such times, their holiness would come from the Mystery itself.[4]

The question remains: Are the gods and goddesses real in this way? Are they real ontologically as well as experientially? From the vantage point of an ecological spirituality, we can go either way. Those who travel the ecological path can, if they choose, believe in the ontological reality of gods and goddesses, all the while remaining Christian, or they can remain, as I do, undecided. In order to attend to other gods and to learn from them, we need not assume that gods and goddesses have ontological reality as inhabitants of a spirit world, though we may assume this if our perception of the evidence suggests it. We need only recognize that they have independence from our conscious egos. What is important, in other words, is that we recognize their experiential reality for others, and open ourselves to the possibility that they can have experiential reality for us as well.

## The Divine Elephant

In order to open ourselves to this possibility, an analogy from Hinduism can help. The analogy is that of an elephant being touched by blind people. According to the analogy, the divine Mystery is like an elephant, and we are like blind people touching various limbs of it, offering different descriptions relative to what we are touching. As we offer our descriptions, we often fail to realize that we are describing different features of the same reality from different points of view. The result is often religious intolerance. The point of the analogy is to remind us that oftentimes, in our alternative descriptions of the divine Mystery, we are apprehending the same reality from different points of view.

The ecological spirituality I am suggesting in this work will add a new twist—and perhaps a Christian twist—to the analogy. It will say that the elephant is itself in process, along with the blind people touching it, and that it adapts itself to the needs and circumstances of the people doing the touching. It is not that the blind people are touching a passive elephant; rather, it is that the elephant itself is reaching out to be touched. It is an incarnational elephant, an elephant who seeks to become enfleshed in people's lives. Indeed, the elephant is within our own imaginations, beckoning us to touch it and then to imagine it in ways appropriate to our needs and circumstances. Just as Jesus offered his own body for our internalization, so the divine elephant offers its own limbs for our imaginative apprehension. Its limbs are themselves aspects of itself, aspects of the divine Mystery.

Given this analogy with its incarnational twist, the gods and goddesses of the world's religions, including Christianity, can be understood as points of contact with the elephant. The gods and goddesses, including god the father, are *limbs-as-touched*. Let us first explore the way in which they are "limbs," and then turn to the significance of the qualification "as touched."

As limbs, the gods and goddesses embody aspects of the Mystery itself. They are part of the very life of the Mystery, which is to say that the Divine is actually within our imaginations in the form of divinities. As limbs of the elephant, these divinities can be understood, at least in part, as ways in which the Divine adapts itself to the needs and circumstances of human imaginers. For people who suffer, the Mystery becomes a vulnerable god, a fellow-sufferer whose presence is felt in the imagination; for people who need hope, the Mystery becomes a future god, a coming messiah; for people who need to laugh, the Mystery becomes a co-laugher, a cosmic trickster; for people who need to feel linked with nature, the Mystery becomes an earth goddess, or an animal, or, like the Greek god Pan, partly human and partly animal. Individuals and societies can be prompted by the divine lure of the Mystery to imagine the Mystery itself in any or several of these forms, and the forms themselves may then reveal and embody some aspect of the Mystery. As limbs of the elephant, the gods and goddesses represent one of the Mystery's ways of approaching human beings. The lure of the divine Mystery is, among other things, a lure to open ourselves to new images, and in so doing to imagine and enflesh the Mystery.

And yet the gods and goddesses are not simply limbs of the elephant *per se*, they are limbed *as touched*. To touch something is to add part of oneself to the item touched. It is to apprehend it from a particular point of view, in a particular historical circumstance, with particular preconceptions, and with particular interests. This means that the gods and goddesses do not simply disclose the Divine, they also embody our own projections onto the

Divine, our own approaches to, and interpretations of, its nature. Sometimes these interpretations may well be misinterpretations. We might even miss the elephant altogether. Some feminists believe, for example, that the image of the Mystery as heavenly father reveals nothing of the Mystery except male projection. My suggestion is that, at the very least, there is some projection in patriarchal imagery, and in feminist imagery as well.

From the fact of projection we rightly realize that we cannot and should not absolutize any image of the Divine, including the image of a heavenly father. In this context, to "absolutize" an image is to construe it as a final, definitive revelation of the divine Mystery, and to deem it uncriticizable. The contemporary resistance to experimentation with alternative images of the Divine in the Christian church is an example of such absolutization. Absolutization is problematic because it so often leads to dominating others, including the earth and other animals, in the name of holy revelation. It neglects the fact that, even though almost all gods and goddesses embody some aspect of the Divine, none do so without an addition of human projection and none exhaust the mystery of the Holy.

Given the risk of absolutization, we might be tempted to do without the gods and goddesses altogether. We might say, for example, "Why not get rid of all imagery, all divinities, and just speak of the Mystery?" There are two reasons why this is inadvisable.

First, gods and goddesses can be beautiful in their own right, helpful in attuning us to the rest of creation, and revelatory of the divine Mystery. To abandon the world of imagery in the name of more rarefied abstractions such as "the Mystery" is to abandon one of the richest dimensions of a shalom-filled existence.

Second, such abandonment is ultimately impossible. In fact, we never encounter the divine Mystery except through points of contact. We never encounter the elephant except by touching its limbs. These limbs may be human or nonhuman images, but they can also be more abstract and rarified concepts, such as "the supreme being" or "the first cause" or, to use concepts employed in this essay, "the divine Lure" or "the heart of the universe." Any concept or image of God is, in its own way, a god or a goddess. It is a finite object of the psyche through which, with the admixture of projection, the divine Mystery is embodied and through which it is beheld. Indeed, I believe that concepts as well as images can be media through which the divine Mystery incarnates itself into our own imaginations. Just as images of personalized gods and goddesses can be media through which the divine is present within us, so abstract ideas can be media. But they are always finite, and we never get beyond them. Even the phrase that I have been using throughout much of this chapter—"the divine Mystery"—is a god of sorts. It, too, is a finite object, in this case more like a concept than an image.

## The Trinity and Polytheism

When we recognize the inescapability of the gods and goddesses as media through whom the divine Mystery can be revealed, it becomes even more important that we learn to affirm them and open ourselves to them. And yet, one of the most difficult obstacles Christians will have in recognizing a plurality of divine faces and voices is our resistance to polytheism. The roots of this resistance are both historical and theological. Historically, our opposition emerged early in Hebrew history when Yahweh was claimed to be the supreme, and then later, the only, divine being. Theologically, our opposition is based on the assumption that worship of other gods is idolatrous: an obstruction of the divine reality's will and an obstacle to earthly well-being. Of course, there is value in this historical precedent and truth in this theological point, a truth to which I will return. Yet there can also be a liability in our disdain for polytheism. Such opposition can lead to an intolerance of others, that is, of those who from our perspective commit idolatry by worshipping what we claim to be "false" gods. Furthermore, it can lead to an idolatry all its own, to a static fixation on our images of the Mystery as the only proper images. Today, for the reasons identified earlier, we need to reconsider our traditional attitude toward polytheism. We need to develop an expanded understanding of the Divine that recognizes truth in polytheistic religious orientations, at least inasmuch as those orientations can suggest that the divine Mystery has many facets, each of which can take the form of a particularized image.

Perhaps we can begin to expand our understanding of the Divine by recalling the traditional doctrine of the Trinity. In this doctrine, however understood theologically, Christians have affirmed that a unique sacred power can be experienced in three distinct faces: that of a father who created the world, that of a redeemer who saved it, and that of a comforter who guides it. In the piety of ordinary Christians, each of these faces has a distinctive voice and mode of presence; each reveals itself in a living image with integrity and autonomy of its own. And yet the autonomy of each member of the Trinity is relational. As is the case with any autonomous reality, the three persons of the Trinity are what they are in and through, rather than apart from, their relations to one another. Each in its own way reveals the unique and ultimate sacred power.

An ecological spirituality can rejoice in this early Christian introduction of diversity into the divine Mystery's unity. The recognition of such diversity enriches our understanding of the Divine and our possibilities for piety. There can be a qualitatively unique piety responsive to the heavenly father in which, for example, the grandeur and majesty of the creator is emphasized in relation to the natural world. There can be a somewhat different piety responsive to the divine son in which the redemptive power of the cross is emphasized in circumstances of guilt, or the ministry of the earthly Jesus is stressed in circumstances of injustice. There can be a still different piety responsive to the holy spirit in which the immanence of the divine within the self and the entire world is enjoyed. While each of these forms of piety might inform a person's life, one or another might be more or less important relative to given needs and circumstances. At one time a person might rightly be drawn to focus on the heavenly father, and at another on the holy spirit. With a divine Mystery whose multi-faceted nature is disclosed in different ways through different internal images, such adaptability is possible and appropriate.

In our time, however, we cannot rest content with only three centers of piety. To limit ourselves to three centers is to suggest, wrongly, that all our needs as Christians—and perhaps by extrapolation the needs of everyone else as well—can be met through relation either to a heavenly father, a divine son, or a holy spirit. A reconsideration of polytheism can lead us to recognize that there may be many more faces of the Divine, many more internal images through which the Mystery can be revealed.[5]

Depending on the needs of the worshipper, some of these additional faces may be young, while others may be old; some may be female, others male; some may be dark-skinned, others light-skinned; some may be friends, and others lovers; some may be human-like and others nonhuman. For Native American Christians, the faces at issue may be from a Native American heritage; for African Christian, from an African heritage; for Asian Christians, from an Asian heritage. What is important is that a given divine face meet the psychological and social needs of the individual devotee as he or she exists in community with others. To the extent that openness to a divine face enhances personal well-being and openness to the earth, sky, and fellow mortals, it can enrich an ecological spirituality.

## The Goddess

A contemporary spiritual movement in which openness to various divine faces does indeed enhance openness to the earth, sky, and fellow mortals is Goddess spirituality.[6] Many of the advocates of this spirituality identify themselves "radical feminists," and they self-consciously distance themselves from the more patriarchal world religions. In the West they speak of themselves as "post-Christian" and "post-Jewish." Clearly, many of us who are Christian have much to learn from the radical feminist movement, not least of which is the fact that one divine person to whom we can and should be open is "the goddess." But perhaps use of a lower case "g" is deceiving. As feminist writers such as Christine Downing, Nelle Morton, Rita Gross, Merlin Stone, Starhawk, Z. Budapest, and Carol Christ use the phrase, "the goddess" is not a face among faces. Rather, she is the Mystery itself as revealed in many different historical images, all of them female-defined goddesses rather than gods. The phrase "the goddess" functions for participants in Goddess spirituality as the word "God" has functioned in previous chapters of this book; as a name for a particularly inclusive and important dimension of the Divine revealed through many different images. The Mystery to which radical feminism points is best written the Goddess with an upper-case "G" than the goddess with a lower case "g."

Is the Goddess "God"? I will deal with this question shortly. For the moment, however, it is important to understand that most advocates of Goddess spirituality would argue that what has been meant by "God," at least as that word has reflected biblical origins, is a distortion rather than expression of the true nature of the Divine. There is certainly truth in their claim. Although there are "feminine" metaphors for the Divine in the Bible and in the Christian tradition, these metaphors have been subordinated to masculine metaphors. The "feminine" has been a male-defined, patriarchal feminine. This subordination reflects the fact that men rather than women have been in control, not only of numerous social structures, but also of mythic imagery. Feminists in the Goddess tradition are correct: in Christian spirituality the Christian's feeling for God has generally been the feeling of a male presence: a heavenly father and that alone.

Two kinds of abuses have resulted from male-centered, or androcentric, spirituality. In the first place, as has been mentioned earlier in the chapter, maleness itself "has been deified as the source of all legitimate power and authority."[7] When God has been male, as Mary Daly has put it, the male has been God. In the second place, an androcentric spirituality has distorted the very nature of divinity, wrongly blocking a recognition of genuinely female-centered, or gynocentric, aspects of the Divine.

How is the Divine conceived gynocentrically, that is, as reflective of women's experience? There is not a single understanding of the Divine to which all radical feminists assent, but many of the writers named above emphasize the following four points.

First, they stress that the Goddess is immanent within the world. Moreover, she is present within with world of nature as well as that of our own psyches. We may experience her differently from the way in which, for example, spiders and leopards experience her. We may experience her as a lure to love, whereas they experience her primarily as a will to live, but all living beings experience and are enriched by her in one way or another. When we are attuned to her, her immanence within nature rightly leads us to affirm, and recognize our inseparability from, the earth and its flora and fauna.

Second, many post-Christian feminists emphasize that the Goddess' immanence within human life (as discovered in dreams, visions, hopes, fears, remembrances, and rituals) leads us to care for others *and* for ourselves. She beckons us, not toward a self-sacrificial love that affirms the world at the expense of the self, but rather toward an inclusive love in which both self and world are affirmed.

Third, they emphasize that attunement to the Goddess results not only in a care for life but also in an acceptance of death, that is, of finitude. We accept this finitude, not because we recognize it is finally overcome by personal immortality, but rather because we see that it is in finitude itself that life's beauty and value is realized.

Fourth, they stress that, though the Goddess is one, she has many different historical expressions, many different faces and voices. A recognition of her many different historical expressions—in various faces and voices—naturally leads to an interest in and appreciation of polytheism. To affirm her reality is to be tolerant of diverse modes of religious consciousness (with the exception of patriarchal modes of consciousness).

Clearly, there is much overlap between the ecological understanding of the cosmic Mystery developed in this essay and the emphases of radical feminists. Both point toward a mode of religious life that has moved beyond sharp dualisms between human and non-human, the divine and the world, life and death. In many respects an ecological spirituality can be enriched by a feminist spirituality. Those of us interested in an ecological spirituality will rightly support and participate in the feminist search for a post-patriarchal world.

Yet we must also recognize that the dissolution of androcentric spirituality in Christianity will not be simple nor quick. It will help, but not suffice, to change language: either by alternating between male and female language, or by seeking gender-neutral language. And it will help, but not suffice, to add certain "feminine" stereotypes to our image of God, thus compensating for the historical projection of male stereotypes.

The problem with these approaches is that the language and stereotypes themselves—women as nurturing, receptive, intuitive, gentle; men as creative, active, rational, and powerful—have been created out of patriarchal social systems. They themselves are in need of transformation. Changing pronouns cannot effect this transformation. What is needed in Christian piety are female personae who can be recognized and worshipped by women themselves as faces and voices of the Divine.

One way to accomplish this is to follow the lead of feminist writers such as those mentioned above. This is to remember and reclaim those female divinities who historically have nourished religious piety, and then, according to disposition and context, to allow them in rituals and meditations to shape imagination and piety in the present. Such divinities include Ishtar from the ancient near East, Isis and Hathor from Egypt, Gaia from Greece, Lakshmi from India, Kuan-yin from China, Amaterasu from Japan, and Oshun from Africa. For women and for men who are thus disposed, these goddesses can be remembered and reclaimed as supplements and alternatives to the exclusive emphasis on male imagery in traditional Christianity. For Christians, this can be to experiment with a worship of the Goddess, understanding her, with her many faces and voices, as a window to the very divine reality disclosed in Jesus Christ. It can be to see Jesus himself as an incarnation, not of a male god, but rather of that feminine spirit whom the Bible names Sophia, or divine Wisdom. It can be to see Jesus as "very Goddess and very man."[8]

As Carl Olson points out, when the totality of the Goddess' manifestations are taken into account, she sharply contradicts existing stereotypes of the female:

> Throughout the course of the history of religions, the goddess has manifested herself in numerous ways. She has been a source of creativity and destruction, a passionate lover and a pure virgin, a temptress and a repeller, beautiful and ugly, terrible and benign. She has been a vivid symbol of fertility, prosperity and wealth, as well as a symbol for loss and death, both beckoning and repulsing the religious devotee. The figure of the goddess as represented in religious history often stands in sharp contrast to the mistaken concept that the feminine is tranquil, passive, or inferior. The goddess is associated with life-giving powers, renewal, rebirth, transformation, and the mystery of death. She also attracts us with her alluring charms, arouses our curiosity about her powers, and tempts us with her pleasureful and unbridled nature.[9]

In fact, so sharply does this Goddess contradict existing stereotypes of the female, that in many respects she reminds us of the very divinity to whom I have been trying to point using the word "God" in this work.

## God and the Goddess

Is the Goddess of radical feminist spirituality identical to the God of an ecological spirituality? So far in this chapter I have, with a few exceptions, avoided using the word "God." I wanted to make the point that there can be many names and images for the divine Mystery, among which "God" is only one. Still, as previous chapters suggest, I believe the word "God" can be used to name the Mystery, and that, given its familiarity and many of its connotations, it needs to be retained within a Christian context. Despite the feminist critique, the word "God," if encountered in different images, including female images, and if supplemented by alternative words, can be freed from exclusively patriarchal connotations. This can best happen if Christians recognize that even "God" is a god of sorts.

To name the Mystery "God," at least as I have tried to use the word in earlier chapters, is to be open to that dimension of the Mystery which lures us toward reverence for all life and which shares in the joys and sufferings of all living beings. It is the Mystery as limitless love. I have suggested that, in the context of an ecological spirituality, this dimension of the Mystery can be encountered through many different images: through the image of a heavenly father, but also that of a cosmic river, a divine mother, a cosmic dancer, an inner light, a universal psyche, an all-embracing heart whose very body is the world. Such images help us to map that dimension of the Mystery in which we can place our deepest trust. They assist us in letting go of all idolatries so as to enjoy a faith without absolutes.

As thus understood, the word "God" points to a set of internal images, each of which can be avenues through which the divine Mystery can become enfleshed in our imaginations. In terms of the elephant analogy, the word "God" points to a particular set of limbs of the divine elephant, specifically those limbs that reveal the elephant's unlimited compassion, its luring power, and its connectedness with the earth, the sky, and fellow mortals. But surely there is more to the Mystery than can ever be captured by the word "God" and its attendant images. There is more to the Mystery than love and co-creative power. Even God must be understood as a divinity of sorts, an aspect of the Mystery, perhaps its very heart, but not the Mystery as a whole.

The same obtains, I believe, for the Goddess. As feminists use the word, it points to that set of limbs in the divine elephant which enables women to affirm themselves as women, and which simultaneously invites them to affirm the earth and its living inhabitants as manifestations of holy power. Like "God," "the Goddess" seems very much connected with eros, with care, with compassion. This suggests that "the Goddess," too, is a divinity of sorts, an inclusive reality that includes within itself many aspects of the divine Mystery, many but not all the limbs of the divine elephant.

Clearly, some of the limbs to which I have been attempting to point with the word "God" are limbs to which radical feminists are also pointing with the word "Goddess." Perhaps, in our time, the divine Mystery is itself becoming enfleshed in different people's imaginations both through God, ecologically understood, and the Goddess, relative to the needs of the people at issue.

In time, the two divinities, God and the Goddess, may even coalesce, such that they will be equivalent names for one another. Perhaps in time both will be imaged, sometimes with the help of one name, and sometimes the other, as a cosmic Heart in whom all things are appreciated in their intrinsic value, and as an inwardly felt lure by which all things are beckoned toward the fullness of life relative to the circumstances at hand. In the distant future, Christian worship may use both words—"God" and "the Goddess"—to name a presence who is strong, but in a caring rather than a coercive sense; who is tender, but in a sense that does not exclude powerful activity; who is erotically and compassionately attractive, but in a way that does not exclude mystery and awesomeness; who is a catalyst for human liberation, but in a way that does not exclude an intimate connection with the whole of nature and a concern for its liberation from human exploitation; who is transcendent, but in a way that is deeply embodied in the world; who is immanent within all life, but in a way that does not exclude human and other creaturely freedom; who is is the very eros of female sexuality, but also the eros of authentic male sexuality as well. In this work I have tried, and will continue to try in what follows, to use the word "God" in a way that indicates this kind of divine presence.

For the foreseeable future, however, most of us in Christian communities had best recognize that God and the Goddess are two distinct ways in which the one divine Mystery can be felt. Obviously these divinities can point to, and bring into our lives, overlapping dimensions of the Mystery. But for far too long "God" totally supplanted "the Goddess" in societies influenced by Christianity. Imagistically, the Goddess herself needs time, much time, to reassert her power in her own right before any talk of her "resemblance to God" is in order. Ecological Christians can rightly recognize that there can be truth in both images: that God *and* the Goddess are divinities through whom the divine Mystery becomes incarnate in our imaginations. An ecological Christianity is, after all, a Way that excludes no ways.

## Choosing Divinities in Light of Shalom

Of course there are limits. Not all the faces and voices we discover within us are theophanies of the Divine. I have already suggested that the images of the Mystery as a cosmic policeman who inspires fear, or as an all-powerful puppeteer who causes or permits tragedy, are deeply problematic, that they are more projective than revelatory. No doubt our psyches include many divinities that are not divine disclosures. Sometimes we hear voices that call us toward a destruction of ourselves and others, either through jealousy, resentment, or sheer hatred. Sometimes we see faces that are but mirrors of our own egos, idealized images of our private or class self-interest. If by openness we mean trust in faces and voices as revelations of the Divine, we cannot be open to all the gods and goddesses.

As Christians, the criteria by which we distinguish which gods and goddesses we might be open to, and which not, is shalom, the fullness of life as discussed in Chapter One. Those gods and goddesses to which, in our best judgment, openness yields shalom in relation to ourselves, fellow creatures, and the earth can in fact be trusted as theophanies of the divine. Openness to such gods and goddesses is not only spiritually satisfying and personally fulfilling, it offers promise for that justice and sustainability which, as discussed in the first chapter, is our best hope.

To accept this criterion is not to have privileged access to the Divine. It may be the case, after all, that the Divine is anti-shalom, and that the criterion of shalom is partial or wrong. On matters of faith, no certainty is possible. To accept shalom as a criterion for evaluating various claims to theophany is itself to trust in one face and voice of the Divine—one theophany—as normative for the evaluation of others. This is the face and voice of Jesus Christ, not as he was in himself—for no one, not even Jesus, exists in isolation—but rather as he emerged out of prophetic Judaism, as he has been interpreted by biblical witnesses, and as he can be interpreted by us today. The very meaning of Jesus is in process.

In the context of this work, to take Jesus-as-interpreted as normative is to do two things. First, it is to see Jesus as one whose life, death, and resurrection were witnesses to shalom. He may not always have embodied shalom, but he seems to have hoped to do so. To take Jesus as normative is to take up his cause—his yearnings for shalom as symbolized in the phrase "kingdom of

God"—as our own.

In addition, it is to see in the circumstances of his life and death the voice of the Mystery made concrete, the Word made flesh. Here the "Word" means the lure of the Mystery. To say that in Jesus we see the Word made flesh is to say that in his actions and yearnings we see the Lure embodied. In the man Jesus—including his hopes and dreams as well as his actions—we discover the Mystery in a way that is decisive for our own self-understanding. This is not to say that Jesus was a supernatural being. He was, as tradition has often said, fully human. Rather, it is to say that in his humanity he sometimes opened himself to God in such as way that his hopes and God's yearning became two sides of a single life journey. He became transparent to God's Lure in such a way that God's Lure became his lure.

Christians who interpret Jesus as the Word incarnate need not think that all significant truths about God were or are exhausted by Jesus. They need not say, for example, that Jesus was as awakened as was the Buddha, or that he had as adequate an understanding of the good society as did Muhammad, or that he was as mystically attuned as was Sankara, or that he saw as deeply the implications of patriarchy as does Mary Daly. Nor need Christians say that all gods and goddesses were replaced or supplanted by Jesus' own experience of God as father. Truths and gods *not* known by Jesus or by Christians in the past can indeed by appropriated, creatively transforming contemporary Christian consciousness. Christians need only attend to those truths and insights, that, to the best of their knowledge, enrich the truth and hope of shalom as revealed in Jesus.

If, then, by openness to the gods and goddesses we mean trust in them as faces and voices of the Divine, then we can trust them inasmuch as they enrich and supplement that commitment to shalom we see in Jesus. In closing, however, it is important to note that "openness to the gods and goddesses" can have other meanings. It can mean awareness of, and attention to, gods and goddesses not for what they teach us about the Divine, but for what they teach us about ourselves. And all do indeed teach us something about ourselves, for all are within us as part of us, and all involve our own projections. If this is what we mean by openness, then we can and should be open to all the gods and goddesses, including those who call us toward destruction and those mirror our own self-interest. For only in being aware of all the gods and goddesses that we can best understand ourselves, and thus understand what obstructs our capacities to be open to the Lure. In this second sense of openness—openness as awareness of the gods and goddesses as aspects of our own psyches—Christianity is indeed a Way that excludes *no* ways. Openness to the gods and goddesses—all of them—brings us toward that self-understanding which is itself a feature of, and a contribution to, shalom.

## Questions for Reflection and Discussion

1. Examine your own assumptions concerning the meaning of the word "reality." From your perspective are the images that appear in dreams "real"? If not, why not? If so, how does their reality differ from that of the physical world? If so, are they less real or more real than the physical world? Than God?

2. How do you experience the image of a "heavenly father"? As authoritarian? Caring? Both? Neither? Is this image one from which you are alienated or one in which you find meaning? What social factors incline a person to find this image meaningful? What social factors lead to an alienation from the image?

3. Consider what this chapter calls "the polytheistic consciousness." What relation do you see between this consciousness and the general emphases of an ecological spirituality? Can a spirituality be truly ecological that does not partake of such consciousness?

4. Imagine that you are charged with developing a religious education program for young children in a Christian church,

and that part of your task is to introduce them to the mythologies of the world religions. A girl asks if one of the goddesses of ancient Egypt was as real as the biblical Yahweh. How would you answer her question?

5. Do you understand and appreciate why some feminists insist on referring to the divine Mystery as Goddess rather than God? In your view, can Christians learn to think of the Mystery as a Goddess, all the while remaining Christian; or is Goddess imagery inherently incompatible with authentic Christian faith? Explain your answer.

6. Do you think it possible for Christians to pray to the Mystery conceived as Krishna? As Kali? As Shiva? Can they do so and remain true to the Christian faith? Or must they simply reflect upon such imagery from a distance, fearful that actual prayer would be too intimate a relation with a false god or goddess?

7. How, in your view, can Christians distinguish between false gods and true gods? What are the most influential idols of our times? Many have suggested that they are not inward archetypes but rather outward allegiances such as material success and national security. Do you agree? Why or why not?

# Openness
to People

In July 1988, I visit-
ed what has been called the world's most polluted city: Cubatao, Brazil, just south of São Paulo. I went there with a group
sponsored by the World Council of Churches to study the response of Brazilian churches to environmental crises.

The air of Cubatao is polluted by noxious and toxic gases that
spew from petrochemical industries owned by multi-national
corporations, whose managers live outside the city in cleaner
air. The multinationals are in Cubatao and in other such cities in
Brazil because there they have cheap labor and few regulations.
Because of the gases released night and day by the factories of
Cubatao, the surrounding mountains have been almost totally
denuded of vegetation. Even the industrialists are afraid of land-
slides that might harm their factories. But the true victims are
the poor of Cubatao, many of whom have been displaced by the

factories, and who have been forced to move into ghettoes in swamp ground. These poor breathe the poisonous air almost continually. In their ghettoes, there is no plumbing. Urine runs into the swamp from each house; feces are dumped into holes. Much of the water is filthy, the result of factory waste as well as human waste. Cubatao is not a pleasant place.

I remember meeting a mother and son who lived in one of the ghettoes. The son was about a year old at the time, the very age of my own son, Jason. I noticed a multitude of red spots on both their faces. I was told by one of our guides that such spots were common among the poor in Cubatao, the result of the air they breathe. Such spots are often symptomatic of a type of cancer, I learned, from which the poor suffer—a result of toxic substances. I realized that the boy had not half the chance to survive that Jason had, and that the mother had not half the chance to survive that I had. I thought of this mother and her son later that day as we, members of the World Council study group, got back in our bus and went to the more pleasant surroundings of a seminary in São Paulo. To this day I wonder if they are alive.

The visit to Cubatao vividly reminded me of something I realize daily as I see homeless people, prostitutes, drug addicts, and lonely elderly in cities in North America, and as I read about abused children, terrorism, violence, political prisoners, and the hungry in the newspapers. It is this: openness to the earth, sky, gods, and *nonhuman* mortals is not enough. An ecological spirituality must be radically open to *human* mortals, including the woman and her son in Cubatao, lest it become mere ecological fascism or spiritual self-indulgence. Not least, it must be sensitive to the poor and powerless, recognizing that as long as anyone is broken in body and spirit, so are we all, because our lives and theirs are bound together, whether we know it or not.

In identifying with the poor and powerless, an ecological spirituality aligns itself with the basic themes of liberation theologies. It will add to these themes a concern for liberating *all* life, but it will in no way deemphasize the theme of liberating *human* life. It will see that the ways of thinking and feeling which have led to an oppression of the earth and other animals are the very ways of thinking which also lead to an oppression of people.

This chapter is divided into three sections. In the first, I discuss what it can mean from an ecological perspective to say that humans are made in the image of God. In the second, I discuss openness to fellow humans as a form of listening to one another. In the third, I discuss openness as a response to the need of others to participate in the decisions which directly affect their lives.

## Made in God's Image

Among the millions of species that have been called into existence by God, we humans seem endowed with capacities for care and responsibility that are, for the most part, unparalleled on our planet. It seems that we can love more deeply and sin more disastrously than most other animals, and that, in communion with one another, we can enjoy types of intimacy, and suffer types of estrangement, many other animals will never know. Our uniqueness is itself the result of hundreds of thousands of years of hominid evolution, in which God has been present, working with the situations at hand, beckoning us to become more and more aware of our own possibilities and responsibilities. While our uniqueness does not make us more loved or less "natural" than other creatures, it does make us different.

A spirituality of ecology must take note of this difference. It can do so by creatively interpreting the biblical idea that humans, and humans alone, are made in the image of God (Genesis 1:26f). In the biblical context, it is not clear what the image actually is, for its nature has been diversely interpreted throughout Christian history. The *imago dei* has sometimes been identified with free will, sometimes with qualities of the soul, such as simplicity and immortality, and sometimes with human reason.[1] More often than not, it has been understood as that which makes humans not only different from, but superior to, the rest of creation.

An ecological spirituality will reject any interpretation of *imago dei* which stresses human superiority. While the richness of experience enjoyed by human beings and other highly sentient creatures may enrich God's own life to a degree greater than that of many other creatures (one-celled organisms, for example), there is little point in emphasizing this. Given our contemporary need to overcome that ethical dualism which claims that only humans are worthy of moral regard, it is more important in our time to emphasize the fact that all creatures add something to the divine Life. Ecologically oriented Christians recognize that God loves all creatures equally; God fully empathizes with each creature on its own terms, cognizant of its unique needs, perspectives, and values for itself.

In an ecological context, then, what can it mean to say that we are made in the image of God? Given that we are the product of evolutionary processes, both cultural and biological, it can mean that we are capable of mirroring the divine Consciousness in a way heretofore unparalleled on the planet earth. The possibilities of which I am speaking are not for intelligence or imagination, important as they are. Other creatures are intelligent and imaginative in ways that may well supersede our own. Rather, the possibilities of *imago dei* are for an inwardly felt affection—a care—that can enrich our intelligence and imagination, and that can inform our actions. To be made in the image of God is to have within ourselves possibilities for care that approximate the divine care.

There are several types of care toward which we are called, and which together form the image of God within us. The first is *inclusive care*, that is, an inwardly felt care that extends to each and every creature, that is appreciative of that creature's otherness and mystery, and that seeks the well-being of that creature. Tragically, this care is perpetually frustrated by realities of moral and natural evil. As we see from predator-prey relations, life is robbery; one creature takes the life of another, and violates its interests in surviving, in order to survive itself. Nevertheless, we humans are lured to recognize that each life—that of the malarial mosquito who preys upon the infant, and that of the infant whom the mosquito infects—is important in its own right. We are invited to see, and moreover to feel, that each life is intrinsically valuable, that each life matters to itself, and hence to us and to God. Squirrels, cats, porpoises, and chimpanzees may not be called toward such care, but we are. When we respond to possibilities for inclusive care, we are responding to the image of God within us.[2]

The second type of care toward which we are called, and which is part of the image of God within us, is *just care*. A just care is one that recognizes the urgent need within human communities around the globe for economic equity, political participation, and personal liberty. In communities that are just, people are free from poverty, unemployment, and hunger; they are free to participate in the decisions by which their lives are affected; and they are free to dissent, to choose religions and philosophies of their own, to seek and obtain information, and to travel. To even the most casual reader of the daily newspaper, the contemporary needs for justice should be clear. These needs are appropriately underscored by liberation theologies from Asia, Africa, and Latin America; by black, Hispanic, and feminist theologies in North America; and by political theologies from Europe. These theologies rightly insist that the divine beckoning is not simply for inclusive care, important as it is, but also for a just care: a care for those whom Jesus called "the least of these," and who today form the majority of the world's population.

A third type of care is *intimate care*. Whereas a just care can be exercised in relation to those whom we might not directly know, intimate care requires direct contact with a beloved person. It is affection for, tenderness toward, and deep understanding of another person on a one-to-one basis. While some may enjoy approximations of this type of intimacy with nonhuman creatures, for example with companion animals, most of us know it or seek it most deeply in relation to other humans: parents, children, friends, and lovers. In intimate care, we are allowed to feel other people with a depth that resembles God's own care for all creatures.

Two further points can be made about the nature of, and relationship between, intimacy and justice. The first is that intimacy is qualitatively richer than justice. Imagine a wife and husband, living in an urban/industrial setting, active in church affairs and in the life of their community. They are "model Christians," they embody a Christian commitment to justice in their own marriage, sharing responsibilities in common, allowing each other personal freedom to develop as individuals, and making decisions jointly. They are actively engaged in projects aimed at the betterment of their societies, with particular focus on the poor. They live modestly, at a level at which others in the world could live without depleting the world's resources. By most measures, such a couple would enjoy the fruits of justice, and would themselves be living justly inasmuch as they seek to promote it for others.

Yet, and herein lies the difference between intimacy and justice, something may still be missing in their relationship. They may still be individuals isolated from one another, devoid of mutual trust and shared ecstasy. If he is typical of many male over-achievers, the husband may not really listen to his wife when she speaks. He may be easily distracted, or simply take her for granted. If she is typical of many female victims of male over-achievers, the wife may rightly feel that her husband does not really know her as a friend, or as a lover. Two people may live justly, but not intimately. In immediate relationships, openness involves more than justice. It involves trust and ecstasy, including sexual ecstasy. It involves intimate care.

A second point is that justice is an enabling and sometimes indispensable condition for intimacy. The very way in which we approach our intimates is made possible by, and has implications for, the relative justice or injustice of the social systems in which we live. I am able to share responsibilities with my wife, and she with me, because we live in societies, and are members of social classes, in which employment is possible. The fact that we are employed and hence that we have food, clothing, shelter and other comforts sets the stage for other forms of intimacy and openness to one another. Those without employment and without the basic necessities of life, owing to the unjust social circumstances in which they find themselves, may not have some of the opportunities my wife and I enjoy. Intimacy may involve more than justice, but it does not involve less. The approximation of some degree of justice in a society is often, but not always, a precondition for members of that society to enjoy certain forms of intimacy. Those of us who enjoy the amenities of justice, and who have special opportunities for intimacy that, for example, an urban youth in a crowded, violence-ridden ghetto may not, have a special obligation to share the fruits of justice with others, including that urban youth. To enjoy intimacy without seeking justice is to miss the mark of responding to God's call for shalom. It is to sin.

In an "ecological" understanding, to briefly summarize, to be made in God's image is to be availed of possibilities for inclusive, just, and intimate care: possibilities which, if actualized, would allow us to mirror God's love in a way that is unparalleled on the planet. As individuals and societies, we continually miss the mark of responding to these possibilities. We are victims and perpetrators of original sin—not in the sense that at one point, in our distant evolutionary past, perfection had been realized, from which our species then fell—but rather in the sense that, as a species, we so persistently "fall short" of our greatest potential. Given data from biological and social sciences, the extent to which our falling short is the result of genetic influences and social conditioning is unclear. What is important is that neither of these influences are utterly determinative. Within us there lies, in addition to these influences, our own capacity to respond to them, and thus partially transcend them, in creative ways. An actualization of possibilities for inclusive, just, and intimate care constitutes one way in which that transcendence occurs.

## Listening to Others

As the discussion of intimacy makes clear, an ecological spirituality is a spirituality that listens. At times, most of us have had the experience of not being listened to, and at times most of us have not ourselves been good listeners. Indeed, some, if not many, of our conversations with acquaintances and friends can take the form of concurrent monologues. [3] As our friends speak to us, either we are so preoccupied with our own agenda and interests that we do not really hear what they are saying; or we have accepted their agenda and interests, but are so busy concocting a response that, again, we do not listen. We fail to hear what they are saying from their *own* point of view, in terms of their *own* interests, on their *own* terms, because we are too preoccupied with our own concerns.

Imagine the alternative: a conversation with someone for whom we are genuine listeners. To hear a woman on her own terms is to imagine ourselves inside her skin, looking out at the world from her own point of view, shaped by the very memories by which she is shaped, and drawn by the very expectations by which she is drawn. We have a feel for the moods, emotions, and ways of thinking which inform her life.

Of course, knowing facts about her can help the listener to empathize with her. It can help to know where she was born, what her life experiences have been, who her friends are, what she aspires to. But deep listening is not an act of knowing *about*. Rather, it is an act of knowing *with*. In genuine listening, the dichotomy between subject and object is eliminated, because at a certain level of the listener's psyche, we "become" the other person, the person listened to. This does not mean that we, as listeners, lack autonomy in our own right; rather, it means that our autonomy is a relational autonomy. It is an autonomy that emerges out of our connectedness with the woman being heard as a creative response to what we are hearing. It does not mean, furthermore, that we necessarily approve of, or agree with, all that is heard; rather, it means that we understand the woman on her own terms. This kind of understanding is analogous to divine understanding. To listen to another person is to feel that person as God feels her, from the inside rather than the outside. It is to hear a person through the heart of God.

The pioneering feminist theologian Nelle Morton speaks of such listening as "hearing into speech."[4] Recounting a consciousness-raising group in which she participated, Morton describes how one woman painfully recalled her life story, guided by the caring, attentive listening of the support group. At one point the woman looked closely at the others and said, "I have a strange feeling you heard me before I started. You heard me to my own story."[5] At this point, says Morton, "I received a totally new understanding of hearing and speaking."[6] Morton saw that genuine listening empowers another person, the one listened to, to uncover depths of experience theretofore unnamed, and in so doing, to speak of those depths freely and openly. By truly listening to others, we "hear others into speech," allowing them to assume more complete, creative control over their own lives.

Perhaps this is how God listens. Drawing upon Morton's insights, another feminist theologian, Catherine Keller, shows how the notion of "hearing into speech" may help us to understand the lure of God in the world and in our own lives. Rather than thinking of the lure as an active intervention in our lives, the will of a domineering power who tells us what to be and do, the lure can be understood as a beckoning into speech, as an act of "hearing into speech" on God's part. Keller rightly points out the problems we face when we find ourselves waiting for an interventionist God to speak and act: "Much faith has been broken in this passive despair, in which one depends upon the Father to take care of us and by His Voice direct us."[7] The alternative, she suggests, is to speak of the lure as emerging out of an all-hearing, divine depth.

> The divine depth, which might indeed hear us before we hear ourselves, would be soliciting our own imaginative response to the total matrix of relational events rather than attempting to persuade us to do an alien will. The lure would be to learn to heed the needs, the sufferings, the impulses and desires configuring our worlds and then to speak for ourselves, to experience the divine wisdom as more curious than directive, as knowingly hopeful but not telling us how to live our lives.[8]

An ecological spirituality can affirm with Keller and Morton that the presence of God in our lives is an empowering presence, one that hears us into speech and that empowers us to hear others into speech. In human life, the activity of God begins not with speaking or telling, but with divine empathy, divine hearing. There is more wisdom in the traditional refrain, "God, hear our prayer" than we at first imagine. This is a way of affirming the primacy of divine hearing.

As Keller points out in proposing that we are lured by God to "heed the needs, the sufferings, the impulses and desires" of other people, a spirituality of listening cannot stop with intimate relations. It is particularly important today that we learn to listen, as best we can, to those whom we know only from a distance. Among other things, it is important that we listen to people of other faiths. Their experiences, too, have something to teach us. From them we learn to relativize our own perspective, better embodying that faith without absolutes discussed in Chapter Two. We see that our way is not the only way. As we listen to some of our co-religionists, as suggested earlier, we may discover truths heretofore unemphasized and perhaps even unrecognized in Christianity.

It is also important that we listen to people without faith, particularly to those, such as some survivors of the Nazi Holocaust, who have ceased to believe in God owing to debilitating encounters with evil. Such listening prevents our faith from lapsing into a sentimental disregard for tragedy, a forgetfulness of evil. It jolts us to recognize that while God's love may be unlimited, God's power to influence the world is partly dependent on the world's response. Even as we affirm that atheists may be right, that in fact there may be no God at all, we nevertheless risk trusting that there is a God, one who cannot prevent all tragedy, but who can indeed suffer with those who suffer, and offer possibilities for wholeness out of chaos.

But listening to the pain of others is not enough. Amid our openness to others, both intimate and distant, we must also learn to listen to joy. Sometimes this is more difficult. Often we can share in the suffering of others because it gives us a sense of control, relief, or companionship. Misery loves company. It is more difficult, it takes a larger heart, to share in the joy of others, particularly if such joy is foreign to our own experience. Here, too, openness to the inner prompting of God can help. For God's life is one that includes the joy as well as the suffering of others, and God's call is for us to share in this inclusive spirit. In so doing, the image of God within us becomes, in its own small way, a likeness of God. We become participants in the divine life, experiencing that love without jealousy which characterizes God's own care for the world. This unjealous love is itself freeing. Our own envy becomes divine care.

## Respecting the Need to Participate

Whether listening to the joy or to the suffering of others, Christians are especially attuned to the needs of others to freely participate in the world, that is, to realize their own creative potential for enjoying rich relations with other people, the land, plants and animals. An ecological faith is one that sees all things as interconnected, as parts of one another. One way or another, every person on earth is already connected to the earth, sky, gods, and mortals. But the way in which a given being is part of the web of existence makes all the difference. It is particularly important that people be able to participate constructively, in ways partly chosen by themselves, in the immediate webs of which they are a part. As much as is possible, it is important that they choose the gods and goddesses most meaningful to them, the land into which they sink their cultural roots, the animals and plants with whom they will have their deepest affinity, and the people with whose destinies they will most intimately share. An ecological spirituality will seek ways of freeing people to choose their own ways of being related to the world, their own modes of connection.

In so doing, however, an ecological spirituality will not lapse into the illusion that freedom is itself absolute. It will recognize that human beings, like other mortals, are instances of what Buddhists call *pratitya-samutpada*, or dependent origination. This is to say that we are historical beings, that we are shaped by traditions for good or ill. We are not free to be unrelated to the world; rather we are free to be richly related to the world. The freedom we seek for ourselves and for others and toward which we are beckoned by the indwelling Spirit, is to participate with quality and in ways that empower us, and others as well, to be partial agents of our own destinies, to be subjects rather than objects of history.

Consider those who are unable to participate with quality: for example, the woman I met in Cubatao, Brazil. Suffering from a terminal illness caused by unclean water and air, she is indeed connected to a web of social and environmental existents which are part of her very being. Her life vividly exemplifies *pratitya-samutpada*. She is connected to the world, however, in ways that are destructive and imposed. In the simple act of breathing, she is connected to earth through toxic wastes, spewing from petro-chemical factories owned by multinational corporations, that enter her lungs. She is also connected to the sky through diminished hopes for her children, to the gods through the image of a divine father who (so some have told her) wills her suffering as a test of her faith; and to mortals, including other people, who share her fate.

Or consider a man in the United States who has been driven off his farm, and from small-scale, labor-intensive agriculture, by the capital-intensive monoculture of the corporate farm, and who now stands in an unemployment line. He, like the woman in Cubatao, is profoundly connected to a web of social and environmental influences which have become part of his very being. He, too, is linked with the earth, sky, gods, and mortals. But neither of these two people are active participants in shaping the circumstances by which their lives have been affected. Rather than being subjects of history, they are victims of history, objects of fate. An ecological faith will be particularly attuned to the need of people to be subjects of their own lives and thus to be co-creators in community with one another, with the rest of nature, and with God.

Indeed, from an ecological perspective, the more just and sustainable the community in which a person dwells, the greater that person's opportunities for co-creation. Sometimes, of course, the aims of co-creators in a given community will conflict. This is not necessarily bad. In societies that are socially just, ecologically sustainable, and spiritually satisfying, humans will disagree, and some of this disagreement will be part of the very richness of shalom. But an ecological spirituality is premised on the idea that the deepest need of people is not to exercise their creativity at the expense of others, but rather to do so in cooperation with others. In genuine community, we creatively choose and accept dependency on others, cognizant of our limitations as well as our strengths. As M. Scott Peck puts it in discussing the lure within each human being for individuation:

In this individuation process we must learn how to take responsibility for ourselves....Yet the reality is that there is a point beyond which our sense of self-determination not only becomes inaccurate and prideful but extremely self-defeating. It is true that we are created to be individually unique. Yet the reality is that we are inevitably social creatures who desperately need each other not merely for sustenance, not merely for company, but for any meaning in our lives whatsoever. These, then, are the paradoxical seeds from which community can grow.[9]

To Peck's important insight, however, an ecological spirituality will add this note: the community to which our hearts most deeply aspire, and in which shalom is most fully realized, is one that includes cooperative relations, not only with other people, but also with the earth and other animals. We ourselves become fully human inasmuch as we enjoy rich relations with our mother the earth, and with our relatives the plants and animals. A community that excludes the earth and other animals from its horizons of care is not a full community.

But even this is not enough. Most deeply, our hearts desire communion not only with the earth and its living inhabitants, but also with the sky. We desire communion with the unfolding cosmos of which we are a part, and with myriad hopeful possibilities—for life on earth and life beyond earth—that we discover within our own imaginations as we gaze into the heavens. A community that excludes the cosmic context of terrestrial existence, that forgets our relation to the stars and heavens above, is, like the one that forgets the earth and other animals, not a complete community.

And even this is not enough. Our hearts also desire communion with the world of spirits. Many humans the world over have sought, and continue to seek, cooperative relations with departed ancestors. Their "communities" include the dead as well as the living. "Ancestor worship" is particularly characteristic of primal religions in Africa and Asia. Sometimes these people have been criticized by Western Christians as being "superstitious," if not also "idolatrous" in their concerns. An ecological Christianity will reject such insensitivity. It will be respectful of the fact that departed ancestors are certainly "real" for those who venerate them, even if invisible to the scientific eye. And it will be open to the possibility that ancestors continue to exist in a spirit world, that they can be communicated with, and that they can be viable members of a living community. It will recognize that many human members of a community can be invisible rather than visible, but nevertheless present.

In the previous chapter, however, I stressed an additional dimension of the spirit world to which an ecological spirituality will also be open: the realm of the gods and goddesses. The divinities, I said, are those imaginatively apprehended presences through whom we discover the divine Mystery, and through which the Mystery itself becomes incarnate in our own imaginations. When freed of elements of projection, they include the heavenly father of traditional Christianity and the gynocentric Goddess of feminist spirituality; the animal-like divinities of ancient Egypt, and the androgynous divinities of Hinduism. In the last analysis, our hearts desire reconciliation with these presences as well. A human community that excludes the spirit world, including the internal world of gods and goddesses, is, like one that excludes the earth and sky, not a full human community.

In a word, the community we seek as people is a community of the earth, sky, gods, and mortals: a community of the fourfold. From an ecological perspective we find God, and our place within God's life, inasmuch as we find our place within the fourfold. For most people, this search for a home in God's life is an ongoing pilgrimage. Inasmuch as we are open to other people, we are open to their possibilities for finding a gentle, fitting habitat within the fourfold. This is to allow them to enjoy rich relations with their portion of the earth, with their vision of the sky, with their understanding of the gods and goddesses, and with their friends and relatives, human and nonhuman. It is to encourage them to live compassionately in relation to their fellow sentient beings, and openly in relation to their own divine-ly-inspired possibilities for well-being. It is to recognize that their way may not be our way, and that this is all right. Inasmuch as we serve people in this way, helping them to find community in the fourfold, we serve the very spirit in whom we, as Christians, place our deepest trust, the living Christ. If they know we are Christian, they will know it not by our dogmatism or arrogance, but by our openness, our care, our joy.

## Questions for Reflection and Discussion

1. Some people who are deeply concerned with the poor emphasize social justice over any concerns with the earth and other animals. They feel that moral energies are depleted if we add "the earth" and "other animals" to our concerns. How might those who seek to embody an "ecological spirituality" respond to this charge? Is their response justified?

2. How have you understood the claim that people are made in the image of God, and how does this understanding differ from that proposed in this chapter? What strengths do you find in this chapter's proposal? What weaknesses?

3. Can it ever be true to say that God is made in the image of people? If God is made in the image of people, who does the making? Review the proposal in Chapter Six that God responds to the needs of people, and then explain your answer. Can it ever be true to say that God is made in the image of animals and the earth as well? Review the proposal in Chapter Three that God responds to the needs of other animals, and then explain your answer.

4. What are the differences between just care, intimate care, and inclusive care? Do you think these forms of care can fuel one another? Can they ever work at cross purposes? Explain your answer.

5. Review the concept of participation developed in this chapter. In what ways are people in your own community able to

participate meaningfully in the decisions by which their lives are affected, and in what ways are they not? What is being done in your community to remedy the latter?

6. Consider people who talk all the time and rarely listen, and compare them with people who listen all the time, and yet who are never heard. What social circumstances contribute to the former, and what to the latter? In your view, is listening to others the luxury of people in power, or is it relevant even to those whose primary problem is not being heard?

7. How might the theme of listening be relevant to prayer? From the ecological perspective developed in this work, does God listen to prayer? If so, how might God respond?

# Conclusion

## A Way That Excludes No Ways

I have proposed that an ecological faith will "hear" others into speech, heeding their need to participate freely in the decisions by which their lives are affected and to enjoy community with the earth, sky, gods, and mortals.

It is with the enjoyment of community that, for the Christian, the church can enter. In a Christian context, the church can be one place, perhaps for some even the most meaningful place, to enjoy such community. This community can be experienced in the warmth of fellowship and in mutually undertaken acts of service. It can also be experienced in worship services. In celebrating the eucharist, for example, we can celebrate our community with other people and we can simultaneously anticipate the community of shalom for which we yearn for all people and for the whole of nature.

Indeed, in the simple act of eating bread and drinking wine, we can understand ourselves as intimately connected to the earth, sky, gods, and mortals. In eating the bread we commune with the earth as the very substance we are eating; with the sky whose rain and warmth nourished the wheat from which the bread has been made; with other mortals, including those people whose labors have tilled the soil, harvested the wheat, and made the bread, and including those plants and animals that supplied nutrients for the wheat; and with God, who is present in the bread itself, in our memory of Jesus, and in the dinely infused images—the divinities—within our own hearts and imaginations. The eucharist, enjoyed freely and in a spirit of love, offers a distinctive opportunity for Christians to feel the presence of the earth, sky, gods, and mortals.

In all honesty, we must acknowledge that the church is a very long way from becoming a genuine stimulus for ecological thinking and feeling. This is particularly the case with the North American church. In many respects the North American church—whether Catholic, Protestant, or Orthodox—is still very much a conduit for the *status quo* rather than a home for the poor and powerless; an enemy of all that is nonhuman rather than a friend of the earth and other animals; a haven of exclusivism and parochialism rather than a Way that excludes no ways. For my part, I have not given up on the church, and I hope it does not give up on me. I need it for the many graces it offers, and for the fellowship it brings me. But I do not find the church an easy place to live out an ecological spirituality. I find myself hoping that, despite current trends, the church can become a nurturer of ecological spirituality. I have written this book with this hope in mind.

By way of conclusion, then, let me summarize the basic characteristics of an ecological spirituality.

1. It springs from a deep-seated hope, not for utopia, but for a more just, sustainable, and spiritually satisfying world.

2. It is shaped by a distinctive way of thinking and feeling: one that emphasizes the interconnectedness of all things, the in-

trinsic value of all life, the continuity of human with nonhuman life, and the compassion of God for all life.

3. It is tolerant and open to other religions, recognizing that much can be learned by Christians from other religions, and that Christianity itself is, or can be, a Way that excludes no ways.

4. It is nourished by a deep-seated faith which sees God as an encompassing Mystery whose love was revealed in Jesus, and who is immanent within each living being as a lure toward wholeness. Influenced by Buddhism, an ecological faith recognizes that neither God nor the world are changeless objects on which to cling. If the word "absolute" refers to a changeless object, then an ecological faith is a faith without absolutes.

5. It employs a pan*en*theistic way of imaging the divine mystery, which means that it images the divine mystery as the mind or heart of the universe, and the universe as the body of God. Just as what happens in our bodies happens in and to us, so what happens in and to the universe happens in and to God. The joys and pains of living beings are shared by God. An ecological spirituality further suggests that things happen in the world which even God cannot prevent. It does not trust God to prevent crosses, but rather to heal and resurrect.

6. It is sensitive to the presence of God as an inward prompting to enter into rich relations with the surrounding world, the outer world and the inner world. An ecological spirituality feels beckoned by God to be open to the entire range of existence: to the earth, sky, gods, and mortals.

7. It seeks to be open to the earth as a living organism having value in its own right as well as value for living beings. It is sensitive to the aliveness of the earth, and to the fact that we are ourselves made of the earth, exemplified among other places by the way in which our own bodies partially compose us. An ecological spirituality is able to feel the body, at least in health, not as an alien force, but as an enfleshment of the sacred earth. It is a spirituality that is able to find God in the joy of dance, the pleasure of food, the quietness of breathing.

8. It seeks to be open to the sky as a realm of possibilities which elicit hope for a more just and sustainable earth and for redemption in life beyond the earth. An ecological spirituality feels the sky as a perpetual reminder that life on earth is itself part of a larger cosmic story, and ultimately, part of a larger divine story. It is infused with a sense of cosmic awe.

9. It seeks to be open to the inward, imagined archetypes within our own psyches: to the gods and goddesses. These archetypes tell us something about the subconscious dimensions of ourselves if not also about the mystery of God. An ecological spirituality recognizes that there are many images through which the divine spirit can be present to the human heart; therefore, while remaining monotheistic, it recognizes the truth of that polytheistic psychology which affirms multiplicity, even in God.

10. It seeks to be open to those mortals who are the animals, our kindred spirits, from whom we can learn about God, in whom God dwells, and toward whom we rightly exercise special care. It recognizes that humans have special responsibilities to respect those animals who have been domesticated for human ends. It also appreciates wild animals. It knows that coyotes, rattlesnakes, grasshoppers, eagles, and cockroaches, too, are subjects of God's unlimited empathy.

11. It seeks to be open to those mortals who are people, in relation to whom we can have our deepest connections, and to whom, in their needs for justice and intimacy, we have our most sacred responsibilities. It recognizes that listening to others is prerequisite to authentic speaking, and that God is one who "hears us into speech." It identifies with the human poor and powerless, recognizing that their poverty and oppression rightly frame a significant portion of the social agenda of a Christian ethic.

12. It refuses to absolutize itself, recognizing that, important as an ecological spirituality can be, it is subject to growth, revision, and criticism. An ecological spirituality sees itself as a pro-

cess of becoming, as a journey. It recognizes that it is in the journey itself, not in a fixed destination, that the fullness of life is discovered.

To the extent that we internalize these twelve ideas into the lived quality of our own experience, we live what I have called an "ecological spirituality."

Mine is not the only possible version of such a spirituality. Other versions are needed in our world, both Christian and non-Christian. Still, the version I have offered is Christian. It is shaped by my own conviction, indebted to Jesus and the Christian heritage, that the divine Mystery is a well-spring of unlimited compassion and a source of life-giving hope for all creatures.

Yet my version is not exclusively Christian. I hope that some of the ideas I have suggested might be appropriated by people of other religious orientations and from non-religious perspectives as well. Indeed, I believe that Buddhists or Hindus, Jews or Muslims, can learn from Christian perspectives, all the while remaining Buddhist or Hindu, Jewish or Muslim. Similarly, Christians have much to learn from these other religions, all the while remaining Christian. If you, the reader, find yourself outside the Christian fold, I hope the ideas have helped you. You need not be Christian in order to live an ecological spirituality.

Nevertheless, you *can* be a Christian and live an ecological spirituality. In this work I have tried to show how. I hope that those of us on Christian journeys—those of us who are what I called "third-phase" Christians in the Introduction—will freely adopt some of these ideas, utilizing them in corporate worship in churches as well as in personal, religious practice. As most of us know, our own tradition is in dire need of creative transformation. No doubt some of the ideas proposed diverge from the Christian tradition. This is all right. Christianity itself is an ongoing tradition capable of growth and change. We best serve Christianity, not by absolutizing the Christian past, but rather by hearing the call of God toward a new and more promising future.

In the last analysis, however, our aim as Christians is not to serve Christianity. Rather, it is to respond to the divine heart: a transcendent yet indwelling Spirit who beckons us toward a reverence for all life, and who calls us to be richly related to the earth, sky, gods, and mortals. As Christians we name this Spirit "the living Christ," because we see the Spirit as having been enfleshed in the ministry of Jesus. We seek to be open to God in our way and our time as Jesus was in his. Some in other religions may have different names for the spirit, and still others may be able to revere life in entirely different ways. We can accept that. Indeed, we can celebrate that. We need not claim that our beliefs are superior to all others, or that ours is the only way. We need only bear witness to the Christ who sets us free to appreciate life in its diversity and fullness.

In our time, then, the way of the living Christ is a Way that excludes no ways. To be an ecological Christian is to live this way, to enjoy its freedom, to partake of its love. It is to feel deeply linked with all that is, with the earth, sky, gods, and mortals. It is to know that that none of us are saved unless all are saved. From an ecological perspective, we are all part of a single web of existence, a dance of life, that is never the same at any two moments, and yet which, in consort with the divine dancer, is all that there is. An ecological Christianity finds salvation in this realization of interconnectedness, itself a gift of God. Our deepest response to this gift is neither complacency nor self-congratulation. It is gratitude. We are grateful to the earth, sky, gods, and mortals themselves, who are part of our very existence, and we are grateful to God, the cosmic dancer, who beckons us to embrace them.

# Appendix

## The Place of Solitude and Silence
## in an Ecological Spirituality

In the preceeding pages I have emphasized that an ecological spirituality is radically open to the entire range of existence. This could suggest, wrongly, that there is no place for solitude in the life of an ecological Christian. On the contrary, solitude can and must play an important role in an ecological spirituality. But the solitude itself must be ecological. It must enrich rather than thwart our capacities for openness to the earth, sky, gods, and mortals.

Solitude is not simply a matter of external circumstances; it is a matter of the heart. Sometimes it helps to isolate ourselves from other people in order to discover our own solitude. In this regard wilderness experiences can be particularly meaningful, for in being alone with nature, we discover aspects of our selves and of nature ordinarily unknown. Our egos are relativized, and our encounter with the wild reminds us how free and awesome are the forces of life and the lure toward life.

Still, it is possible to be alone—solitary in its richest of senses—even in a crowded room. When I speak of an ecological solitude, I am speaking of an inner solitude, one that is experienced regardless of the circumstances in which we are situated. For Christians, the cultivation of solitude and its fruits can be enriched by traditional spiritual practices, such as fasting, prayer, and worship in the context of a local congregation. The enjoyment of ecclesial community can sometimes help rather than hinder a cultivation of solitude. But ecological Christians may sometimes find churches hindrances rather than aids to solitude, in which case other communities must be found. In any case, an ecological Christian will be at home with inner solitude as well as with the surrounding world.

If it is ecological, inner solitude will itself be understood relationally rather than atomistically. If we think of ourselves atomistically, we will imagine that, when we enter most deeply into ourselves, we leave behind our connections with the world. In turning "inward" we leave behind the "outward" behind. An ecological spirituality will recognize the truth in this perspective. We do, after all, block out or disregard certain aspects of the sensory world in moments of extreme solitude. Certain yogic states achieved in the Advaita Vedanta tradition of Hinduism are particularly adept at blocking out sensory input and other forms of worldly influence in order to achieve union with the Godhead, Brahman.

Ultimately, however, an ecological spirituality will be more Buddhist than Vedantist. In the practice of an ecological Christianity, we we will not assume that a discovery of our true selves in solitude reflects a transcendence of all connections; rather we will assume that, when we enter most deeply into ourselves, we find linkages with other realities of which, in ordinary conscious experience, we were for the most part unaware. In solitude we do not find an absence of connections, but rather different kinds of connection. And we gather resources for strengthening our connections with the world. Even in solitude we express, and gather inner resources for, connectedness, or what Buddhists call *pratitya-samutpada*.

But what are these other realities with which we are connected in solitude? And how are we connected to them? Let me name two.

One set of these "inner realities" has already been mentioned in Chapter Six. They are the gods and goddesses, some of whom, as I suggested earlier, are the very faces and incarnations of the divine. Through those apparitions who are agents of *shalom*, we are linked to the Divine; the Divine becomes present to us through the numinous presence of apparitions. Consider the example of Nelle Morton, the feminist theologian quoted earlier. As Catherine Keller reports, Morton had a series of visions in the 1970s "that led her to name that Other-in-Self 'Goddess.'"[1] As with other feminists, these experiences emerged in the context of imaginative meditative practices. They deeply affected Morton's life, leading her toward a more complete identification with the women's movement and with the plight of the marginalized in society. Morton became convinced that the Goddess was attempting to usher in a new reality for women, one not at all unlike that just and sustainable society toward which an ecological spirituality yearns. Her Goddess was by no means a sanctioner of the status quo.

Was this Goddess real? For Morton, the Goddess figure who presented herself could not be explained away as a mere dream or phantasy, a mere projection of her psyche. The Goddess was a real presence. And yet Morton did not feel that the Goddess entered her from outside her psychic depths. Rather the Goddess came "up from down under," from depths of a reality within and yet more than her individual self. The Goddess as thus understood is one example of an "other" with whom we may find ourselves linked in solitude.

As certain mystical traditions in both the East and West attest, the divine reality can also be experienced as a reality beyond all images and concepts, in pure silence of the heart. The "God beyond images" is a second type of "inner reality" that can be experienced amid solitude. To experience God in this way is to travel what is sometimes called the apophatic or imageless type of mystical path, as opposed to the kataphatic or imagistic type realized by Nelle Morton. The apophatic tradition is not necessarily biblical, though it has made a valuable contribution to the history of Christian spirituality. Its affect on Christian thinking began in the third century with the influence of neo-Platonic doctrines. Though neo-Platonic ideas fell into disrepute for a time thereafter due to their associations with paganism, they once again achieved prominence in the fifth century through the writings of Dionysius the Areopagite. Through this unknown author, whose mystical theology was taken out of the context of the rest of his work and adopted by numerous Christian thinkers, neo-Platonism shaped the spirituality of such Christian mystics as John of the Cross and Teresa of Avila.

In apophatic traditions, the divine is experienced, not through meditation upon images, but rather through contemplative prayer, a type of prayer which, despite the contemporary connotations of the word "contemplation" as a discursive process, connotes direct intuition beyond all discursion. Here the divine is experienced as an undifferentiated unity—an ocean of pure love, a sea of pure light, a well-spring of pure freedom—in relation to which the finite ego is dissolved, or into which it is absorbed. As Thomas Merton puts it:

> What happens is that the separate entity that was *you* suddenly disappears and nothing is left but a pure freedom indistinguishable from infinite Freedom. Love identified with Love. Not two loves, one waiting for the other, striving for the other, seeking for the other, but Love Loving in Freedom.[2]

Moreover, as the writings of Merton so often make clear, the realization of ecstatic union with divine love is usually experienced as a pure gift, an act of grace, for which a person can prepare, but which he or she cannot produce by her own strength.

Clearly, the kind of "inner reality" discovered amid apophatic mysticism is different from that discovered in kataphatic or imagistic mysticism. The God of the apophatic tradition would not be described as an Other-in-Self, but rather as an Other-into-which-Self-is-Absorbed or as an Other-who-*is*-the-True-Self. Indeed, many apophatic mystics would describe this God as an Other-who-is-not-Other-at-all! And, inasmuch as the word "connection" so often implies two distinguishable realities somehow linked with one another, it may seem inappropriate even to describe the apophatic God as an inner reality to which we are connected in solitude. After all, in the contemplative experience itself, we are not "connected" to this God; rather this God is all that there is.

Still, at least in a Christian context, apophatic mysticism can be understood as relational rather than atomistic in its innermost nature and its results. As the life of Thomas Merton so eminently exemplified, the depths of contemplative prayer can be understood as a realization, not only of our unity with God, but our unity with all other creatures. As Merton puts it: "The more we are alone with God, the more we are united with one another and the silence of contemplation is a deep and rich and endless society, not only with God but with [people]."[3] Or, as William Shannon expresses it in explicating Merton's perspective:

Contemplation is an experience in solitude, but it is not an experience in isolation. My contemplation leads me not only to God but also to other human persons...Meeting others, then, is an aspect of discovering my own identity, because I was never intended to exist in separateness.[4]

An ecological Christian will add that contemplation ought not lead only to an empathetic identification with other persons, but also to a sense of connectedness with the earth and all living beings.

It is noteworthy that an ecological sensibility to nonhuman life was part of Thomas Merton's own spirituality. In *New Seeds of Contemplation* he writes:

The forms and individual characters of living and growing things, of inanimate beings, of animals and flowers and all nature, constitute their holiness in the sight of God....The special clumsy beauty of this particular colt on this April day in these fields under these clouds is a holiness consecrated to God by His own creative wisdom and it declares the glory of God....The pale flowers of the dogwood outside this window are saints....The lakes hidden among the hills are saints....The great, gashed, half naked mountain is another of God's saints.[5]

Here we have openness to mortals, plants and animals included, and to the earth as an integral part of an apophatic sensibility.

Moreover, Merton had a deep sense of the divine lure, which, as shown in Chapter Two, is the very cynosure, the very attractant, of an ecological faith. In the well-known early passages of *New Seeds of Contemplation* Merton writes:

Every moment and every event of every [person's] life on earth plants something in his soul. For just as the wind carries thousands of winged seeds, so each moment brings with it germs of spiritual vitality that come to rest imperceptibly in the minds and wills of [human beings]....The ever-changing reality in the midst of which we live should awaken us to the possibility of an uninterrupted dialogue with God. By this I do not mean continuous "talk," or a frivolously conversational form of affective prayer which is sometimes cultivated in convents, but a dialogue of love and choice....In all the situations of life the "will of God" comes to us not merely as an external dictate of impersonal law but as an interior invitation of personal love....We must learn to realize that the love of God seeks us in every situation, and seeks our good.[6]

As indicated in Chapter Two, an ecological faith—a faith

without absolutes—is precisely this openness to an inwardly felt lure to love. The life of faith does not hold onto God as an object, rather it is an ongoing dialogue of "love and of choice" with an ever-changing and yet ever-faithful lure, through which the living God is present, and which beckons us at all moments, but in different ways relative to circumstance, toward openness to the earth, the sky, the gods, and our fellow mortals.

The point being made here is that the divine lure can also be a lure toward solitude and silence, toward openness to God through images and openness to God beyond images. And it can be a lure for us to respect and appreciate the need of other people, too, to have their own solitude, their own silence, even when their forms of solitude and silence differ from our own. Some of us may be more drawn toward imagistic meditation, some toward imageless contemplation. Some may be drawn toward the divine as Goddess; some toward the divine as "a father in heaven." As long as the fruits of silence are a love of life and a commitment to shalom, there is no reason for Christians to insist that one type of spirituality is higher, deeper, or more revelatory than another. Nor is there reason to say that all people ought to seek guidance through images or through their absence. Christ, after all, is a Way that excludes no ways. Both the kataphatic and the apophatic traditions can be understood as ways in which different people encounter the living reality of divine Mystery and Love. An ecological Christianity is one that respects diversity, indeed celebrates diversity. In the house of the Divine, so it recognizes, there are many mansions.

What is important in our time is that Christians of different orientations unite in our commitment to a world that is more socially just, more ecologically sustainable, and more spiritually satisfying for all people. This does not involve insisting that all people become Christian. Religious diversity is a good to be celebrated. But as Christians we can and should bear witness, in our own lives and hearts, to Christ, to a Way that excludes no ways. In this work I have shown that such a way is one of trust in the divine lure, and one of commitment to the well-being of all life on earth, nonhuman and human. We are able to embody such commitment inasmuch as we are open to the earth, sky, gods, and mortals, and inasmuch as we are open to our own capacities for solitude and silence. The God who hears us into our own speech, I have suggested, is a God who hears us into silence. Amid our silence, we can hear the callings of the whale, the quietness of the dogwood, the rustling of the wind, the hoof-beats of the colt, the crying of the hungry child, and the laughter of the freed slave. These sounds are by no means disconnected from the One in whom we place our trust. They are God's very body. In our silence we are able to hear the voices of God's body as if for the first time, and then to respond with deep, divinely inspired care.

# Notes

## Introduction

1. Dorothee Soelle with Shirley A. Cloyes, *To Work and to Love: A Theology of Creation* (Philadelphia: Fortress Press, 1984), p. 4.

2. Those who enter this third phase "consciously choose religion, but not the village version of it." They attempt to remember the problems of phase one, and they retain the lessons of phase two. They accept the reality of pluralism, realizing that any contemporary religious perspective—including a Christian one—must celebrate rather than reject the reality of pluralism. They acknowledge rather than deny that religion, including Christianity, has sometimes been abusive of life, and that from these abuses Christians must repent. And they accept the tools of critical reason, trying to apply these tools to the very religious way they adopt. They recognize that all religious perspectives, including Christian perspectives, are mythic. They accept myth as myth. With this acceptance, they recognize that myths are stories by which one lives, lenses through which the world is perceived, frameworks and regulative ideals by which experience is organized. Humans do not simply create the fundamental assumptions of their myths, rather they are grasped by them. These assumptions and the myths that contain them come to humans from a realm of the unconscious imagination that partly transcends their conscious egos, and that has its own wisdom. When third-phase Christians return to Christianity, they appropriate Christianity as a set of living myths by which they are once again grasped. For many third-phase Christians the fundamental assumptions by which they are once again grasped include the idea that 1) love is itself a quality of ultimate reality; 2) love in its fullness—including a love of beauty and truth—is the very reality by which life acquires fulfillment and meaning, and; 3) a community in which love rules is worthy of human hope. These assumptions are humanistic, and they may well have been part of the second phase. Yet they are also Christian. Traditionally, the first assumption has been contained in the metaphor that God is love, the sec-

195

ond in the metaphor of Christ as God's son, and the third in the metaphor of the coming Kingdom. Third-phase Christians re-experience the power of these metaphors, accepting and modifying them as living myths, that is, as regulative ideals by which they live. As circumstances require, third-phase Christians may then partially modify the very myths by which they are grasped, changing, for example, the notion of a hierarchical Kingdom to that of a non-hierarchical community, or the notion of a male God to that of a more inclusive God/dess. Such changes are themselves in the interests of that love to which they are committed.

Third-phase Christians realize that the acceptance and partial modification of mythic perspectives is itself characteristically human. They see that myths are inescapable, and that no one, not even those who deem themselves mythless, escapes being grasped by regulative ideals. To celebrate one's mythlessness is itself to be grasped by a regulative ideal, a myth. This is the myth of being in touch with the facts as they are. Part of being a third phase Christian is to be grasped by this ideal. In believing that love is a cosmic reality by which life acquires meaning, and in believing that a community of love is worthy of hope, third-phase Christians also hope that these beliefs are in touch with the way things are. Claiming no certainty or finality of statement, they nevertheless hope that their adopted myth—that there is a loving God, that in Christ this love was shown, and that there is, or can be, a coming Kingdom—is true.

Sometimes this hope for truth, like so many aspects of a religious journey, is grounded in a complex of feelings rather than abstract thoughts. The third-phase Christian's acceptance of myth as myth involves the recognition that there is more to knowing and to life than that critical analysis and skeptical reason acquired in phase two. Religious data are not simply thought about and reflected upon, they are felt and acted out. The religious life involves intuition and feeling, imagination and anticipation, remembrance and touch. Non-intellectual sensibilities are accepted, not as replacements for, but as complements to, critical analysis and intellection.

3. Martin Heidegger, "Building Dwelling Thinking" in *Martin Heidegger: Basic Writings* (New York: Harper & Row, 1977).

4. John B. Cobb, Jr., *Christ in a Pluralistic Age* (Philadelphia: Westminster Press, 1975), p. 22.

## Chapter One

1. Gary J. Coates, *Resettling America: Energy, Ecology and Community: The Movement Toward Local Self-Reliance* (Andover, Massachusetts: Brick House Publishing Company, 1981), pp. 53-85.

2. Walter Brueggemann, "Living Toward a Vision," in Edward A. Powers, *Signs of Shalom* (Philadelphia: United Church of Christ Press, 1973), p. 101. Quoted in Wesley Granberg-Michaelson, *A Worldly Spirituality: The Call to*

*Take Care of the Earth* (San Francisco: Harper & Row, 1984), p. 74.

3. These two values have been identified and explained by L. Charles Birch and John B. Cobb, Jr. in their pioneering work on the interface of theology and biology, *The Liberation of Life* (New York: Cambridge University Press, 1981). See pp. 234-265. In articulating an ethic of life, Birch and Cobb note the words singled out by the World Council of Churches as expressive of the most important aspects that need to be promoted for human societies in the contemporary world. The words the World Council chose were "just," "participatory," and "sustainable." For the sake of simplicity, Birch and Cobb reduce these three words to two—just and sustainable—believing that participation is itself included within justice.

4. Birch and Cobb, *The Liberation of Life*, p. 245.

5. Of course, a good deal more needs to be said concerning the "nuts and bolts" of a just and sustainable world. In a global village that is both just and sustainable, technologies are appropriate to the needs of people, and to the limits and rights of nature. Sometimes these technologies may be "high" and sometimes "low." In communications, for example, high technologies may well be in order if they facilitate global interaction and do not destroy cultural diversity. In agriculture, simpler technologies may be in order, technologies that preserve the topsoil and can be easily employed by rural peoples, thereby enhancing their own economic well-being. In energy production, the "soft energy paths," such as wind, water, and solar power, may be preferable to the "hard paths" of nuclear power and fossil fuels that dominate the technotopian scenario. For one thing, the soft paths are more conducive to democratic control or participatory justice. As we move into the future, we are rightly lured by the image of a world that is in may ways "technological," but employs technologies appropriate to the interests of justice and sustainability. We cannot determine in advance the exact character of the local, human communities of which a just and sustainable global village will consist.

Generally speaking, a human community is any group of people bound together by common economic, political, cultural, religious, or philosophical interests. In today's world, communities of this sort include ethnic groups, economic classes, religious fellowships, nation-states, and multinational corporations. Many people participate in several at once. For example, a peasant woman in Guatemala may participate in a local village community in which she sells and barters goods, a religiously-inclined "base-community" in which she regularly explores the social implications of biblical religion, a national community of fellow Guatemalans, and an international community of fellow Roman Catholics. Each of these communities is "local" in the sense that it is part of her own "local" self-understanding, and in the sense that, viewed in the context of the global whole, it is specific rather than general, particularized rather than universal. This does not mean that they are bad. They are both good and necessary. They give the woman's life its depth and meaning, as do analogous forms of community in all our lives. Perhaps they contain the seeds of the kinds of local communities that a global village will need.

6. For a discussion of the intrinsic value of nonhuman nature and the rights of nonhuman life see Birch and Cobb, *The Liberation of Life*, pp. 141-176.

7. See Birch and Cobb, pp. 144-175, for the development of a process "ethic of life."

8. Wendell Berry, *The Gift of Good Land* (San Francisco: North Point Press, 1981), p. 181.

## Chapter Two

1. David L. Shields, *Growing Beyond Prejudices: Overcoming Hierarchical Dualism* (Mystic, Connecticut: Twenty-Third Publications, 1986), p. 163.

2. Holmes Rolston, *Environmental Ethics* (Philadelphia: Temple University Press, 1988), p. 25.

3. Shields, *Growing Beyond Prejudices*, p. 232.

4. Alfred North Whitehead, *Process and Reality* (New York: Macmillan, 1978), p. xiv.

5. Quoted in Wesley Ariarajah, "Religious Plurality and Its Challenge to Christian Theology," *World Faiths Insight*, 1988, 19, p. 4.

6. For information write: Society for Buddhist-Christian Studies, Graduate Theological Union, 2400 Bridge Road, Berkeley, CA 94709 USA.

7. Buddhist emptiness can be, and has been, interpreted in many ways. My interpretation draws from at least two sources. The first in Frederick J. Streng, *Emptiness: A Study in Religious Meaning* (Nashville: Abingdon, 1967). The second is T. Kasulis, *Zen Action/Zen Person* (Honolulu: University of Hawaii Press, 1980).

8. John B. Cobb, Jr., "Buddhist Emptiness and the Christian God," *Journal of the American Academy of Religion*, 45 (1977): 11-25.

9. Quoted in Huston Smith, *Beyond the Post-Modern Mind* (New York: Crossroad, 1982), p. 120. Originally in "Can a Christian Be a Buddhist, Too?" *Japanese Religions*, 10 (December 1978): p. 11.

## Chapter Three

1. Much of the discussion of contemporary animal abuse that follows, unless otherwise documented, is a paraphrase of a report prepared by an ecumenical team for the World Council of Churches at a consultation sponsored by the Church and Society Sub-unit of WCC held in Annecy, France, in September 1988. I was a part of the team, as were approximately fifteen other theologians from different parts of the world, including Korea and Africa. In some instances the phrases I use to describe animal abuse in this

chapter—or put into the mouth of the hypothetical woman—are the phrases of the as yet unpublished report. These phrases are my own, since I was one of the report's authors, though they certainly belong to the other authors as well. All of us at the conference were indebted to one of our fellow participants, the animal rights philosopher Tom Regan, for offering a first draft of the section of the report dealing with questions of animal abuse, and for apprising us of so many areas of animal abuse. Through Regan's guidance, all participants at the consultation agreed that Christians need to attend to the abuse of individual animals under human subjugation at the same time that they attend to problems of injustice and violence among humans and exploitation of the earth. Though "Annecy Report" has not yet been published, excerpts have appeared in newspaper articles in various parts of the world and in the magazines *The Animal's Agenda* (April 1989) and *The Animal's Voice* (July 1989), both published in the United States. Plans are being made for the report in its entirety to be included in an anthology of essays on ecological theology to be edited by Charles Birch (who was also at the consultation), William Eakin, and me. This book will be published by Orbis Books. For information concerning the report, contact the Church and Society Sub-unit of the World Council of Churches, 150 Route de Ferney, P.O. Box 66, 1211 Geneva 20, Switzerland.

2. With slight modification of language, the following description of the Draize Test is borrowed from Henry Spira, "Fighting to Win" in *In Defense of Animals*, ed. Peter Singer (New York: Harper & Row, 1986), p. 194.

3. "Annecy Report" (see endnote 1)

4. *Ibid.*, p. 13.

5. Most of the information supporting the argument for vegetarianism comes from John Robbins, *Diet for a New America* (Walpole, N.H.: Stillpoint Publishing, 1988).

6. Quotations from Tom Regan are from an article called "Christianity and Animal Rights: The Challenge and the Promise," presented at the Annecy Consultation (see note 1).

7. *Ibid.*

8. "Annecy Report" (see note 1).

## Chapter Four

1. Norman Meyers, ed. *Gaia: An Atlas of Planet Management* (New York: Anchor Books, 1984), pp. 122-123.

2. *Ibid.*, p. 158.

3. *Ibid.*, p. 158.

4. *Ibid.*, p. 159.

5. *The Diaries of John Ruskin*, ed. Joan Evans and John Howard Whitehouse (Oxford, The Clarendon Press, 1956-59), XIX, p. 362.

6. For a study of Ruskin's animism, see John D. Rosenberg, "The Geo-

poetry of John Ruskin," *Etudes Anglaises*, Vol. XXII, No. 1 (1969), pp. 42-48. My attention to this passage in *The Ethics of Dust* is indebted to Rosenberg's article.

7. Alfred North Whitehead, *Process and Reality*. Corrected Edition edited by Donald Sherburne and David Ray Griffin (New York: MacMillan, 1987), p. 167.

8. Barrett, *The Illusion of Technique*, pp. 363-364.

9. *Ibid.*, p. 365.

10. *Ibid.* pp. 368-369.

11. *Ibid.*, p. 369.

12. Quoted in Birch and Cobb, *The Liberation of Life*, p. 248.

13. C. Dean Freudenberger, *Food for Tomorrow?* (Augsburg: Minneapolis, 1984), p. 15.

14. Lester Brown, *State of the World* (New York: Norton, 1985), p. 228.

15. David Katz, "Sustainable Agriculture: Basic Guidelines for Future Farming," *In Context: A Quarterly of Humane Sustainable Culture*, Vol. 8, Winter 1984, pp. 37-39.

16. *Ibid*, p.38

17. *Ibid*.

18. *Ibid*.

19. H. Wheeler Robinson, *Inspiration and Revelation in the Old Testament* (Oxford: Clarendon Press, 1946), p. 13.

20. Quoted in Granberg-Michaelson, p. 16.

21. Also Leopold, *A Sand County Almanac and Sketches Here and There* (New York: Oxford University Press, 1968), p. 221.

## Chapter Five

1. Walter Brueggemann, *The Prophetic Imagination* (Fortress Press: Philadelphia, 1978).

2. H. Paul Santmire, *The Travail of Nature: The Ambiguous Ecological Promise of Christian Theology* (Philadelphia: Fortress Press, 1985), pp. 17-29.

3. *The Prophetic Imagination*, p. 13.

4. Sallie McFague, *Metaphorical Theology: Models of God in Religious Language* (Philadelphia: Fortress Press, 1982), p. 163.

5. Elie Wiesel, *Night* (London: Bantam Books, 1960).

6. *Ibid.* , pp. 61-62.

## Chapter Six

1. This is taken from an actual account noted by J. Baird Callicott in *In Defense of the Land Ethic: Essays in Environmental Philosophy* (New York: State University of New York Press, 1989), p. 188.

2. Ibid. p. 188.

3. John Hick, *God Has Many Names* (Philadelphia: Westminster, 1980).

4. Of course, if gods and goddesses are real in this sense, they, like us, would be partly dependent on other things, including perhaps our own beholding of them. They would be part of that vast cosmic network I have called the earth, the sky, the gods, and fellow mortals. From an ecological perspective nothing, not even the divine Mystery itself, is absolutely self-contained.

5. To recognize more faces may, of course, be to contravene the traditional doctrine of the Trinity. But it need not do so. Those committed to the doctrine of the Trinity may interpret additional faces of the Divine as different manifestations of one or another of the Three Persons. What is important, one way or another, is that Christians move toward an enriched, multi-faceted monotheism in which new divine faces can be recognized and affirmed.

6. See, for example, *Weaving the Visions: New Patterns in Feminist Spirituality*, ed. Judith Plaskow and Carol P. Christ (San Francisco: Harper & Row, 1989), p. 96-169.

7. Carol Christ, "Symbols of Goddess and God in FeministTheology," *The Book of the Goddess Past and Present: An Introduction to Her Religion*, ed. Carl Olson (Crossroad: New York, 1985), p. 235.

8. See James M. Robinson, "Very Goddess and Very Man: Jesus' Better Self," in *Encountering Jesus: A Debate on Christology* (John Knox Press: Philadelphia, 1988), p. 111-122.

9. Olson, *The Book of the Goddess: Past and Present*, ix; ii.

# Chapter Seven

1. *The Oxford Dictionary of the Christian Church*, edited by F.L. Cross, second edition edited by F.L. Cross and E.A. Livingstone (Oxford University Press: Oxford, 1974), p. 692.

2. Chapter Three showed what this care will involve in relation to plants and animals; Chapter Four in relation to the Earth. Chapter Five (Openness to the Sky) showed that care may also issue into a hope that in some plane of existence, if not our own, the tragedies of this life may be reconciled, such that each creature, given its needs and interests, can realize its potential. An inclusive care begins with a recognition that the needs and interests of each and every creature on and beyond earth are important in their own right.

3. I am grateful to Sheila Davaney of Iliff Theological Seminary in Denver, Colorado, for this insight.

4. Nelle Morton, *The Journey Is Home* (Boston: Beacon Press, 1985).

5. *Ibid.* p. 127.

6. *Ibid.*

7. Catherine Keller, "Goddess, Ear, and Metaphor: On the Journey of

Nelle Morton." *Journal of Feminist Studies in Religion*, Vol. 4, No. 2 (Fall, 1988).

8. *Ibid.*, p. 65.

9. M. Scott Peck, M.D. *The Different Drum: Community Making and Peace* (New York: Simon and Schuster, 1987), pp. 54-55.

## Appendix
1. Keller, "Goddess, Ear, and Metaphor," p. 71.

2. Quoted in William E. Shannon, *Thomas Merton's Dark Path* (New York: Farrar, Straus, Giroux, 1987), p. 50.

3. Quoted in Shannon, p. 43.

4. *Ibid*, p. 42.

5. Thomas Merton, *New Seeds of Contemplation* (New York: New Directions) 1972, p. 30.

6. *Ibid*, p. 14.

# Selected Bibliography

Those interested in further reading may find the two lists below helpful. The first consists of books in process theology. The second is a list of additional readings relevant to an ecological spirituality which emphasize readings relevant to an openness to the earth and to animals.

*Further Readings in Process Theology:*

Birch, Charles and Cobb, John B. Jr. *The Liberation of Life: From Cell to Community.* Cambridge: Cambridge University Press, 1981. Critiques the mechanistic paradigm that prevails in the life sciences and includes an explanation of a more "ecological" way of understanding life. Demonstrates the connection of this new way of understanding life to a liberation of the poor and oppressed, the environment, and nonhuman animals.

Brock, Rita Nakashima. *Journeys by Heart: A Christology of Erotic Power.* New York: Crossroad, 1988. A powerful articulation of a radical feminist vision using process points of view.

Brown, Delwin. *To Set at Liberty: Christian Faith and Human Freedom.* Maryknoll, New York: Orbis Books, 1981. Develops a theology of freedom by forging a partnership between process theology and Latin American liberation theology.

Cobb, John B. Jr. *Christ in a Pluralistic Age.* Philadelphia: Westminster Press, 1975. Important book that explains how Christianity can be understood as a "way that excludes no ways," all the while remaining faithful to Jesus of Nazareth. Difficult reading for a non-academic audience, but nevertheless worthwhile.

_____. *Process Theology as Political Theology.* Philadelphia: Westminster Press, 1982. This book is particularly helpful for those interested in overlap of and difference between process theology and European political theologies, both of which seek to be in communication and solidarity with liberation theologies. Particularly helpful in showing relevance of ecological perspectives to liberating thinking.

_____. *Beyond Dialogue: Toward a Mutual Transformation of Christianity and Buddhism.* Philadelphia: Fortress Press, 1982. Good demonstration of the mutually-educational dialogue between Christians and Buddhists. Includes a discussion of faith without attachment such as that proposed in Chapter Two.

_____. *Praying for Jennifer: An Exploration of Intercessory Prayer in Story Form.* Nashville: The Upper Room, 1984. A good book for senior high school students, introducing process theology in the context of discussing intercessory prayer.

Cobb, John B. Jr., and Griffin, David R. *Process Theology: An Introductory Exposition.* Philadelphia: Westminster Press, 1976. A basic introduction to process theology, though written in a somewhat technical style. Many who read this book will find that a background in philosophy is necessary for complete understanding.

Daly, Herman, and Cobb, John B. Jr. *For the Common Good: Redirecting the Economy Toward Community, the Environment, and a Sustainable Future.* Boston: Beacon Press, 1989. This book is particularly helpful for those interested in the economic implications of ecological thinking. Shows that concerns for social justice and ecological sustainability can coalesce.

Davaney, Sheila Greeve, ed. *Feminism and Process Thought: The Harvard Divinity School/Claremont Center for Process Studies Symposium Papers.* Lewiston, New York: Edwin Mellen Press, 1981. One of the first books to systematically explore connections between process and feminist thought.

Griffin, David Ray, ed. *The Reenchantment of Science.* Albany: State University of New York Press, 1988. Part of a series in what Griffin and others call "constructive postmodern" thinking. The introductory essay by Griffin is helpful for understanding the relation between process theology and what has come to be called "postmodernism."

_____, ed. *Spirituality and Society: Postmodern Visions.* Albany: State University of New York Press, 1988. An important series of essays on ecological spirituality and the quest for a postmodern worldview.

_____. *God and Religion in the Postmodern World.* Albany: State University of New York Press, 1989. An excellent explication of a process point of view and its relevance to issues of peace, science, and spirituality. The sixth chapter of Griffin's book contains a sustained defense of the possibility of life after death, a theme which I develop briefly in Chapter Five.

_____, ed. *Varieties of Postmodern Theology.* Albany: State University of New York Press, 1989. Positions process theology within the broader movement of "postmodern" Christian thinking.

_____, ed. *Primordial Truth and Postmodern Theology.* Albany: State University of New York Press, 1989. A dialogue between Griffin and Huston Smith, the latter a well-known interpreter of world religions and an articulate advocate for a return to pre-modern "perennial" religious and philosophical points of view.

_____, ed. *Sacred Interconnections: Postmodern Art, Spirituality, and Political Economy*. Albany: State University of New York Press, 1990. Includes essays by several process theologians, plus an important essay by Joanna Macy, a Buddhist thinker who amplifies some of the points advocated in Chapter Two.

Hartshorne, Charles. *Beyond Humanism*. Lincoln: University of Nebraska Press, 1968. Important demonstration that "humanism" can itself be an obstacle to ecological thinking.

Keller, Catherine. *From a Broken Web: Separation, Sexism, and Self*. Boston: Beacon Press, 1986. A visionary work exploring the interface of process and feminist theology. Difficult reading but quite worthwhile.

McDaniel, Jay. *Of God and Pelicans: A Theology of Reverence for Life*. Philadelphia: Westminster /John Knox, 1989. Deals with relation of God to violence in nature; the theoretical foundations of a respect for life and environment; aspects of an ecological spirituality (some of which are not dealt with in *Earth, Sky, Gods, and Mortals*); and the relevance of feminist theology to the quest for an ecological Christianity. Those interested in connections between feminism and ecological spirituality may find the final chapter of this work particularly relevant.

Muray, Leslie A. *An Introduction to the Process Understanding of Science, Society and the Self: A Philosophy for Modern Humanity*. Lewiston, New York: Edwin Mellen Press, 1988. An excellent accessible introduction to the practical implications of process theology for a broad range of issues, from education through politics to science.

Pregeant, Russell. *Mystery without Magic*. Oak Park, Illinois: Meyer-Stone Books, 1988. This is an excellent book for newcomers to process theology. Highly recommended as a text for undergraduates and adult classes in religious education. Introduces process theology in the context of discussing the nature and relevance of faith to the modern world. Good in its display of connections between process and biblical points of view.

Suchocki, Marjorie Hewitt. *God-Christ-Church: A Practical Guide to Process Theology*. New York: Crossroad, 1982. Just what the title says, a practical guide to process theology. Good at showing connections between process theology and classical Christian doctrines such as atonement and Trinity. Particularly helpful for those who want to learn from process theology, but whose theological orientation is more traditional. Suchocki's style is rich and engaging.

*Resources for an Ecological Spirituality*

Barnes, Michael. *In the Presence of Mystery: An Introduction to the Story of Human Religiousness.* Mystic, Connecticut: Twenty-Third Publications, 1984, 1990. An excellent introduction to world religions and to the nature of religion that can well serve those interested in adopting "a Way that excludes no ways."

Berry, Thomas. *The Dream of the Earth.* San Francisco: Sierra Club Books, 1988. Consists of sixteen esssays by Berry which, taken as a whole, convey his perspective. The best book available for learning about Berry, the most visionary ecological theologian of our time.

Berry, Wendell. *The Unsettling of America: Culture and Agriculture.* New York: Avon/Sierra Club Books, 1978. A classic study of relations between culture and agriculture and of the mentality of exploitation. Extremely well-written.

Callicott, J. Baird. *In Defense of the Land Ethic: Essays in Environmental Philosophy.* New York: State University of New York Press, 1988. An anthology of essays by one of the most influential environmental philosophers of our time.

Carson, Rachel. *Silent Spring.* Cambridge, Massachusetts: Riverside Press, 1962. Classic study of toxic poisoning and its consequences.

Devall, Bill and Sessions, George. *Deep Ecology: Living as if Nature Mattered.* Salt Lake City, Utah: Peregrine Smith Books, 1985. Good explanation of an important movement in environmental philosophy.

Dillard, Annie. *Pilgrim at Tinker Creek.* New York: Harper & Row, 1974. A poetic study by a gifted writer and naturalist. Rich in its explorations of themes related to an ecological spirituality.

Donders, Joseph. *The Global Believer: Toward a New Imitation of Christ.* Mystic, Connecticut: Twenty-Third Publications, 1986. Written particularly for the adult Catholic, this book points toward a new spirituality for the twenty-first century and stresses the relevance of the global village to spiritual concerns.

Durell, Lee. *State of the Ark: An Atlas of Conservation in Action.* New York: Doubleday, 1986. Excellent book for understanding the crises now confronting the earth. Includes discussion of concrete actions people are taking to abate these crises.

Ehrenfeld, David. *The Arrogance of Humanism*. New York: Random House, 1981. An important critique of the ecological irresponsibility of Western humanism.

Eisely, Loren. *The Star Thrower*. New York: Times Books, 1978. A moving writer with training in anthropology and an affinity for paleontology, Eisely's image of a star thrower bears an interesting resemblance to my own image of an all-caring, non-omnipotent God who is on the side of each and every life.

Fox, Matthew. *Original Blessing*. Santa Fe, New Mexico: Bear and Company, 1983. Important explication of a contemporary theological movement: creation spirituality. Has many parallels to the perspective of this book.

Granberg-Michaelson, Wesley. *A Worldly Spirituality: The Call to Take Care of the Earth*. San Francisco: Harper & Row, 1984. A biblically-based evangelical approach to ecological spirituality. An important complement to the less traditional perspective taken in *Earth, Sky, Gods, and Mortals*.

Gray, Elizabeth Dodson. *Green Paradise Lost*. Wellesley, Massachusetts: Roundtable Press, 1979. One of the first and most important demonstrations of links between ways of thinking that oppress the earth and ways which oppress women.

Griffin, Susan. *Woman and Nature: The Roaring Inside Her*. New York: Harper & Row, 1979. A creative account of how attitudes which lead to a human exploitation of the earth also lead to an exploitation of women.

Highwater, Jamake. *The Primal Mind: Vision and Reality in Indian America*. New York: Harper & Row, 1981. Important explication of the significance of native Amerindian perspectives for an ecological worldview and spirituality.

Jackson, Wes, ed. *Meeting the Expectations of the Land: Essays in Sustainable Agriculture and Stewardship*. San Francisco: North Point Press, 1984. Includes essays by some of the most influential and important environmentalists of our time, including Jackson, Wendell Berry, and the Zen-influenced poet, Gary Snyder.

Joranson, Philip N. and Butigan, Ken. *Cry of the Environment: Rebuilding the Christian Creation Tradition*. Santa Fe, New Mexico: Bear and Company, 1984. Good anthology of contemporary versions of Christian ecological theology. Shows the variety of perspectives which can contribute to a reformation of current Christian consciousness.

Leopold, Aldo. *A Sand County Almanac*. New York: Oxford University Press, 1949. A classic study by a mentor of the environmental ethics movement. Develops the concept of a "land ethic" which extends moral consideration to the earth.

Linzey, Andrew. *Christianity and the Rights of Animals*. New York: Crossroad, 1987. One of the most important works in showing how Christians might fittingly embrace the cause of animal rights. An excellent complement to Chapter Three of *Earth, Sky, Gods, and Mortals* on "Openness to Animals."

Linzey, Andrew, and Regan, Tom. *Animals and Christianity: A Book of Readings*. New York: Crossroad, 1988. An anthology of readings in the Christian tradition on animal rights and related issues.

Lonergan, Anne and Richards, Caroline, eds. *Thomas Berry and the New Cosmology*. Mystic, Connecticut: Twenty-Third Publications, 1987. Essays responding to the thought of Thomas Berry, one of the most influential and inspirational of contemporary ecological theologians. Berry is influenced by Teilhard de Chardin, but goes beyond Teilhard in affirming the value of other creatures "for their own sakes."

Lopez, Barry Holstun. *Of Wolves and Men*. New York: Charles Scribner's, 1978. Lopez is one of the most important writers of our time in developing a sense of kinship with, and awe in the presence of, other animals. In this case the animals at issue are wolves. An excellent complement to Chapter Three on "Openness to Animals."

_____. *Arctic Dreams*. New York: Charles Scribner's, 1986. Shows how complex and rich an apparently simple environment such as the Arctic can be. An excellent complement to Chapter Four on "Openness to the Earth."

Lovelock, J.E. *Gaia: A New Look at Life on Earth*. New York: Oxford University Press, 1979. An important supplement to the claim made in Chapter Four on "Openness to the Earth" that the earth itself can be understood as a sacred community. On scientific grounds, it proposes that the earth itself can be understood as a single organism.

McFague, Sallie. *Models of God: Theology for a Nuclear Ecological Age*. Philadelphia: Fortress Press, 1987. Highly recommended for its imaginative discussion of the metaphors of Mother, Lover, and Friend as they might apply to God. Also helpful in its explication of the metaphor of mind and body as applied to God. A good complement to Chapter Two on "Faith Without

Absolutes" and Chapter Six on "Openness to the Gods."

Merchant, Carolyn. *The Death of Nature: Women, Ecology and the Scientific Revolution*. San Francisco: Harper & Row, 1985. Important demonstration of the historical connections between the rise of mechanistic science and the rise of exploitative attitudes toward women and nature.

Morris, Richard Knowles and Fox, Michael W., ed. *On the Fifth Day: Animal Rights and Human Ethics*. Washington D.C.: Acropolis Books, 1978. Good anthology of essays on theological and philosophical approaches to animal rights.

Myers, Norman. *Gaia: An Atlas of Planetary Management*. Garden City, New York: Anchor, 1984. Along with the book by Durell noted above, a good overview of the major environmental crises of our time. Includes recommendations for public policy which would help abate these problems.

Passmore, John. *Man's Responsibility for Nature*. London: Duckworth, 1974. Good survey of the history of Western attitudes toward nature.

Peacocke, A.R. *Creation and the World of Science: The Bampton Lectures 1978*. Oxford: Clarendon Press, 1974. Good for its explication of the mind-body metaphor for understanding God and for showing the way in which this metaphor helps us to interpret God for a scientific age.

Plaskow, Judith and Christ, Carol P., *Weaving the Visions: New Patterns in Feminist Spirituality*. San Francisco: Harper & Row, 1989. Part 2 of this book contains essays that are helpful in understanding the nature of, and motivations for, Goddess spirituality.

Prigogine, Ilya and Stengers, Isabele. *Order Out of Chaos: Man's New Dialogue with Nature*. New York: Bantam Books, 1984. Shows the self-organizing nature of physical systems.

Regan, Tom. *The Case for Animal Rights*. Berkeley: University of California Press, 1983. The most systematic and thorough argument for a respect for animal rights currently available.

_____, ed. *Animal Sacrifices: Religious Perspectives on the Use of Animals in Science*. Philadelphia: Temple University Press, 1986. Offers insights from various world religions which contribute to a respect for animal rights.

Rollin, Bernard E. *Animal Rights and Human Morality*. Buffalo, New York: Prometheus Books, 1981. Easy to read introduction to the cause of animal rights.

Rolston, Holmes III. *Environmental Ethics: Duties to and Values in the Natural World*. Philadelphia: Temple University Press, 1988. Important book by one of the most astute environmental philosophers of our age.

Ruether, Rosemary Radford. *New Woman, New Earth*. New York: Seabury Press, 1975. Shows the relevance of Christian feminist theology to overcoming oppression of the earth, women, and others who are poor and powerless.

Santmire, H. Paul. *The Travail of Nature: The Ambiguous Ecological Promise of Christian Theology*. Philadelphia: Fortress Press, 1985. Excellent survey of the history of Christian attitudes toward nature, showing how they have been both constructive and destructive.

Shields, David. *Growing Beyond Prejudices: Overcoming Hierarchical Dualism*. Mystic, Connecticut: Twenty-Third Publications, 1986. An excellent discussion of the way in which we-they thinking, criticized in Chapter One of *Earth, Sky, Gods, and Mortals,* is a root cause of the many prejudices which oppress people and the earth. Also important in that it links a concern for new ways of thinking with the distinctive insights of liberation theologies.

Singer, Peter. *Animal Liberation: A New Ethics for Our Treatment of Animals*. New York: Avon, 1975. Still one of the most powerful introductions to the animal rights issue. Shocking but effective in its discussions of the abuses of animals in factory farms and scientific laboratories.

Soelle, Dorothee with Shirley A. Cloyes. *To Work and To Love*. Philadelphia: Fortress Press, 1984. Using aspects of process theology, shows connections between oppression of the earth and the oppression of women. Soelle is one of the most gifted and sensitive Christian writers of our time.

Thomas, Lewis. *The Lives of a Cell: Notes of a Biology Watcher*. New York: Viking Press, 1974. Good at showing the "aliveness" of matter, one of the subjects of Chapter Four of *Earth, Sky, Gods, and Mortals*.

World Commission on Environment and Development. *Our Common Future*. New York: Oxford University Press, 1987. Important work, commissioned by the United Nations, that shows links between a destruction of the earth and the oppression of the poor.

Young, Louise. *The Unfinished Universe*. New York: Simon and Schuster, 1986. An interesting and fascinating depiction of the evolutionary process which complements the "new story" described in Chapter Five.

# Index